ADULT PIANO *Adventures*
Christmas

**Arranged by
Nancy and Randall Faber**

AUDIO INCLUDED

We are pleased to include piano recordings of the
selections for study and enjoyment, as well as
orchestrated accompaniments for play-along fun.
Access audio online at
pianoadventures.com/christmas1
password: **gm92y4**

Production Coordinator: Jon Ophoff
Editors: Edwin McLean and Joanne Smith
Illustrations: Terpstra Design, San Francisco
Text Design: Susan Pinkerton
Engraving: Tempo Music Press, Inc.

FABER
PIANO ADVENTURES®
3042 Creek Drive
Ann Arbor, Michigan 48108

ISBN 978-1-61677-370-0

FOREWORD

What is Christmas without Christmas music to fill the season? Whether it be a sacred carol, humorous Santa song or seasonal winter favorite, Christmas music brings joy and meaning to the holidays. **Adult Piano Adventures® Christmas** Book 1 celebrates the holiday season with revered carols such as *Silent Night* and *O Little Town of Bethlehem*, and secular favorites such as *Santa Claus is Comin' to Town* and *Jingle Bell Rock*. Selections include multiple verses—ideal for piano sing-a-longs by the fire or Christmas tree.

This book is designed for adult beginners and for those who have played piano in the past and are reacquainting with the keyboard. Those exploring the piano for the first time will find the arrangements appealing and well within reach. Adults returning to the keyboard can "brush up on basics" with the best songs of the season.

The book is divided into three sections. Section One features easy piano arrangements with minimal hand position changes. Many of the Christmas songs in Section One include an optional duet part. Section Two introduces the I, IV, and V7 chords in the key of C major. With these three chords, a pianist can play countless melodies. Section Three presents the I, IV and V7 chords in the key of G major, with arrangements of *The Little Drummer Boy*, *Trepak* (from the Nutcracker Suite), *Have Yourself a Merry Little Christmas*, and others. The book closes with *Auld Lang Syne* to ring in the new year.

Adult Piano Adventures® Christmas Book 2 offers piano music for the holiday season at an early intermediate level.

Enjoy! May your Christmas season resound with happy musical memories.

TABLE OF CONTENTS

SECTION 1: BEGINNING CHRISTMAS SONGS
Easy arrangements with simple harmonies

SECTION 2: CHRISTMAS SONGS IN THE KEY OF C MAJOR
(with I, IV, and V7 chords)

SECTION 3: CHRISTMAS SONGS IN THE KEY OF G MAJOR
(with I, IV, and V7 chords)

BEGINNING CHRISTMAS SONGS

The first section of this book offers introductory arrangements of Christmas songs with simple harmonies.

ANGELS WE HAVE HEARD ON HIGH (page 8)

The inspiring Gloria chorus harkens back to the medieval custom of shepherds calling to one another on Christmas Eve, proclaiming the joyous birth of Jesus. The melody of an 18th century French popular song was combined with the text of an old French carol to give us the verse we sing today.

AWAY IN A MANGER (page 10)

The original text to this Christmas classic has been adapted to as many as 41 different melodies, though only two Civil War-era strains are in use today. A melody by James Murray (published in 1887) is sung in America, and a melody by William Kirkpatrick (the same melody used for *Flow Gently, Sweet Afton*) is sung in England. The lyric—erroneously attributed to Martin Luther—was taken from a Sunday school book by an unknown author, entitled *Little Children's Book for Schools and Families* (Philadelphia, 1885).

BRING A TORCH, JEANNETTE, ISABELLA (page 24)

The original words and music have been attributed to Nicholas Saboly (1614–1675). This English translation by Edward Cathbert Nunn (1868–1914) communicates the traditions of Christmas in Provence, France in the 1600s. At midnight, people would light torches and walk house to house singing carols and ringing bells. These processions have been compared to torch-light processions that celebrate the Jewish Festival of Lights or Chanukkah.

GO TELL IT ON THE MOUNTAIN (page 26)

The text and tune of this American spiritual was first published in 1909 in Thomas Fenner's *Religious Songs of the Negro as Sung on the Plantations*. The chorus can be sung in one, two, or three parts.

HOME FOR THE HOLIDAYS (page 16)

Perry Como's recording of *Home for the Holidays* was a huge holiday hit in 1954. He recorded the song again in 1959. Both of these recordings were made with Ray Charles and choir. Como's is the most popular version of this Christmas classic and is included in many subsequent compilation albums of his songs.

IT CAME UPON THE MIDNIGHT CLEAR (page 18)

The words were written in 1849 by Edmund Hamilton Sears, a retired Unitarian pastor from Massachusetts. The following year the lyric was adapted to a hymn crafted by Richard Storrs Willis, an editor and critic for the *New York Tribune* who had previously studied music in Europe with luminaries like Felix Mendelssohn, among others.

JINGLE BELLS (page 12)

Although this song has become synonymous with Christmas, it was written in 1857 by James Pierpont for a Sunday school Thanksgiving program at his Boston church and titled "The One-Horse Open Sleigh." The children's performance was so well received that they were asked to repeat it at Christmas time. It has been a Christmas classic ever since.

O COME, ALL YE FAITHFUL (ADESTE FIDELES) (page 22)

The earliest text to Adeste Fideles is found in the manuscripts of John Francis Wade, a scribe at the English college, a seminary for future English priests in pre-revolutionary France. Most of the church documents were destroyed during the French Revolution, and little more is known about Wade. Although the music has been attributed to John Reading, it is not similar to any of his other compositions. Frederick Oakeley first translated Adeste Fideles into English.

O LITTLE TOWN OF BETHLEHEM (page 20)

Phillips Brooks, minister of the Philadelphia Holy Trinity church, wrote this hymn in 1868. Inspired by his visit to the Holy Land, his church organist Lewis H. Redner composed the music at Brooks' request. After meditating on the words for a time, he claims that the tune came to him fully formed and harmonized.

WE THREE KINGS OF ORIENT ARE (page 14)

This selection was written in 1857 by John Henry Hopkins, Jr., an instructor of church music at the General Theological Seminary in New York. The song was created as part of an elaborate Christmas pageant that tells the story of the three Wise Men—Melchior, Caspar, and Balthazar—who came from the East bearing gifts. Their gifts of gold, frankincense, and myrrh signify Jesus' kingship, his oneness with God, and His death on the cross.

WE WISH YOU A MERRY CHRISTMAS (page 6)

This classic Christmas sing-a-long is an example of an old English "waits carol." A "waits choir" was a town chorus of singers who sang at a wide variety of functions and were particularly active at Christmas time. In return for bringing holiday cheer, the singers would receive coins, spiced ale, fig pudding, or roasted pig.

We Wish You a Merry Christmas

Traditional

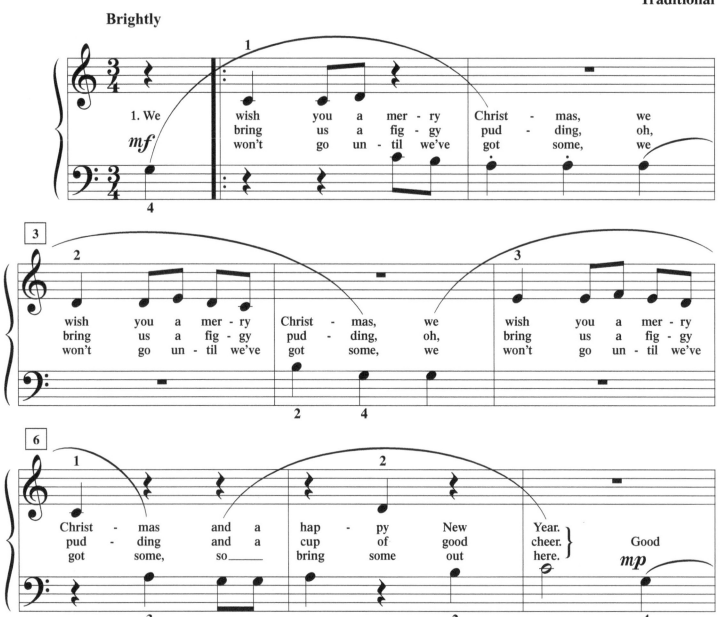

Brightly

1. We wish you a merry Christ - mas, we
bring us a fig - gy pud - ding, oh,
won't go un - til we've got some, we

wish you a mer - ry Christ - mas, we
bring us a fig - gy pud - ding, oh,
won't go un - til we've got some, we

wish you a mer - ry
bring us a fig - gy
won't go un - til we've

Christ - mas and a hap - py New Year.
pud - ding, and a cup of good cheer.
got some, so bring out some here.

Good

Teacher Duet: (Student plays 1 octave higher)

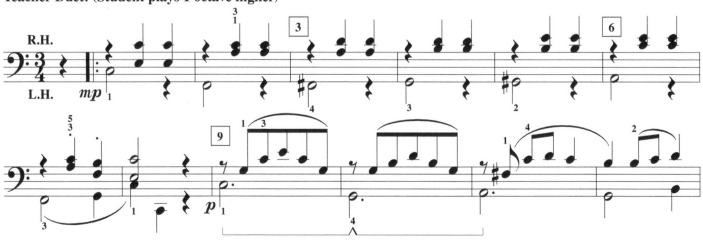

Angels We Have Heard on High

Traditional

Quickly, with joy

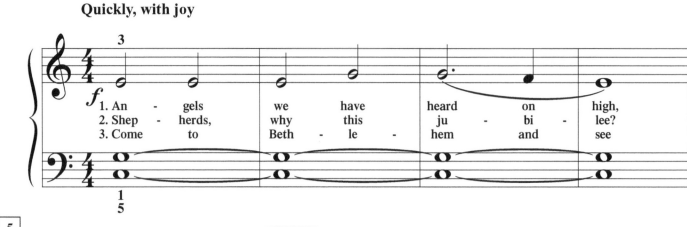

1. An - gels we have heard on high,
2. Shep - herds, why this ju - bi - lee?
3. Come to Beth - le - hem and see

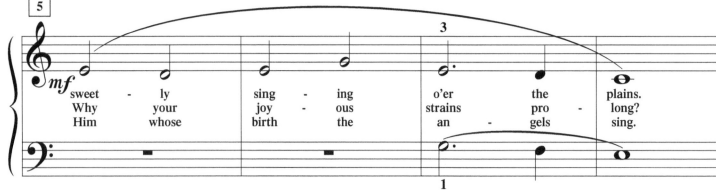

sweet - ly sing - ing o'er the plains.
Why your joy - ous strains pro - long?
Him whose birth the an - gels sing.

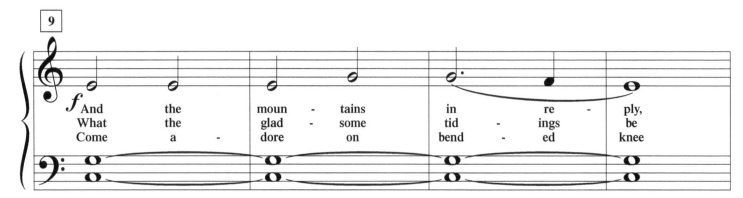

And the moun - tains in re - ply,
What the the glad - some tid - ings be
Come a - dore on bend - ed knee

Teacher Duet: (Student plays 1 octave higher)

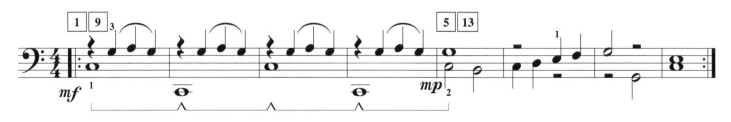

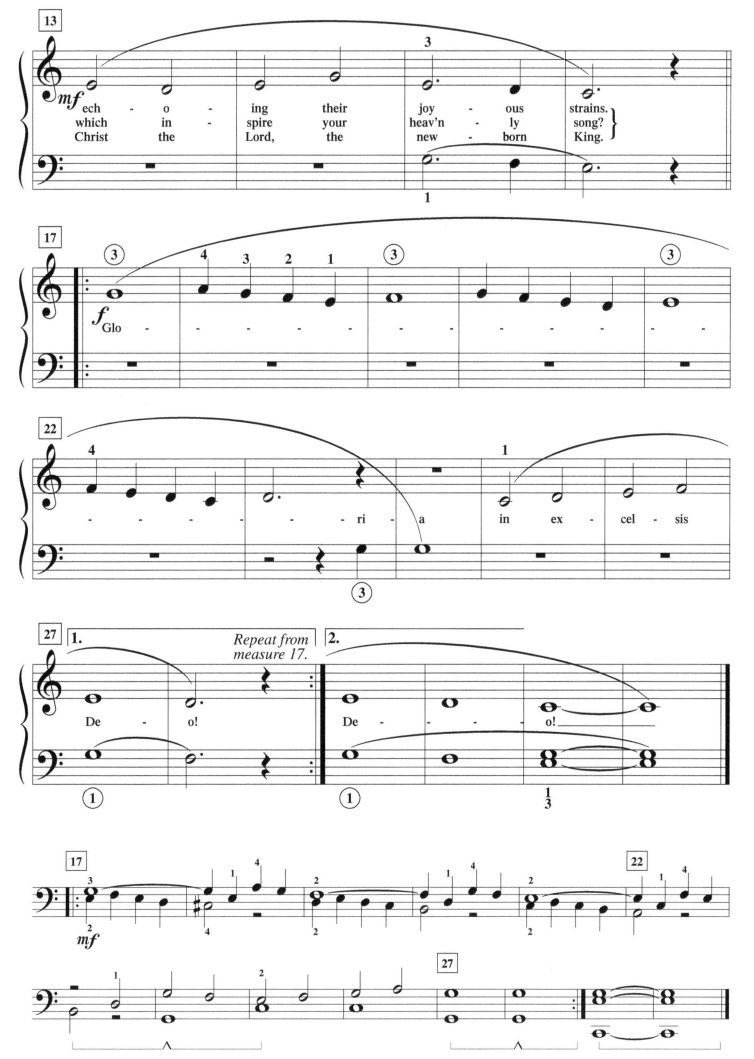

Away in a Manger

Traditional

Moderately

p *L.H. over* *mp*

1. A-way in a man-ger, no
   cat-tle are low-ing, the
   near me, Lord Je-sus, I

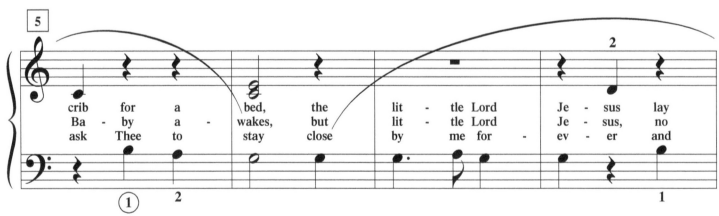

crib for a bed, the lit-tle Lord Je-sus lay
Ba-by a-wakes, but lit-tle Lord Je-sus, no
ask Thee to stay close by me for-ev-er and

Teacher Duet: (Student plays 1 octave higher)

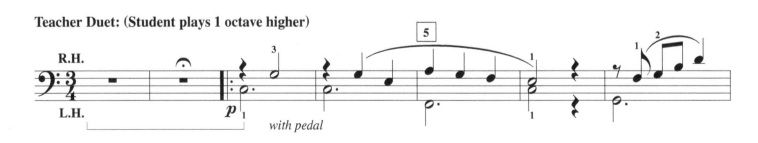

R.H.

L.H.

p

with pedal

Jingle Bells

Words and Music by
James Pierpont

Teacher Duet: (Student plays 1 octave higher)

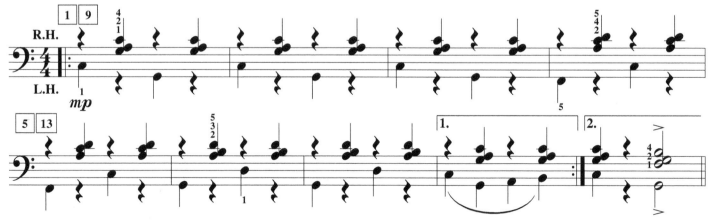

We Three Kings of Orient Are

**Words and Music by
John Henry Hopkins**

Moderately

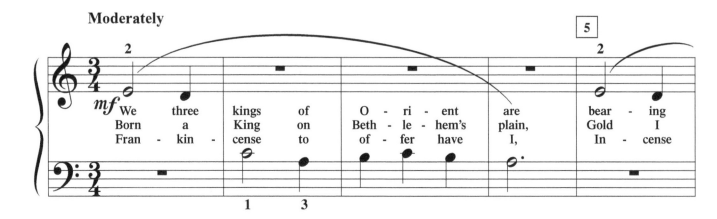

We three kings of O - ri - ent are bear - ing
Born a King on Beth - le - hem's plain, Gold I
Fran - kin - cense to of - fer have I, In - cense

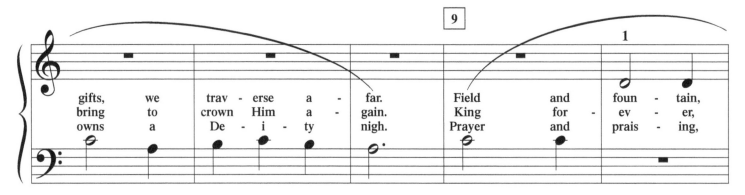

gifts, we trav - erse a - far. Field and foun - tain,
bring to crown Him a - gain. King for - ev - er,
owns a De - i - ty nigh. Prayer and prais - ing,

Teacher Duet: (Student plays 1 octave higher)

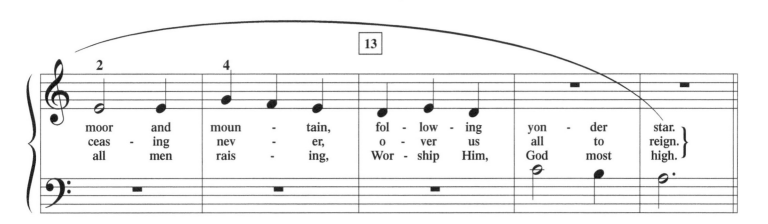

(There's No Place Like)
Home for the Holidays

Words by Al Stillman

Music by Robert Allen

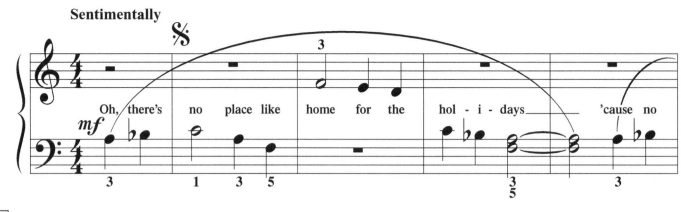

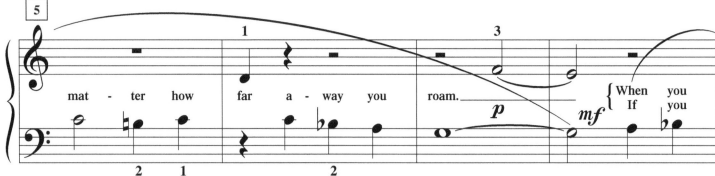

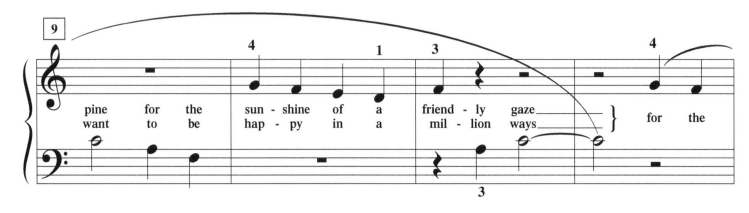

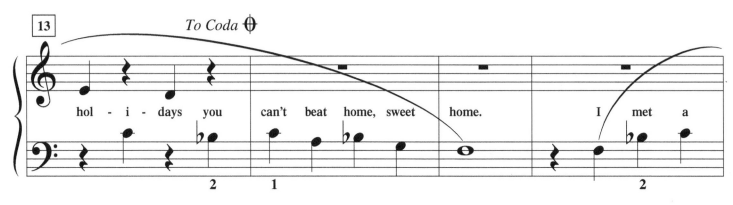

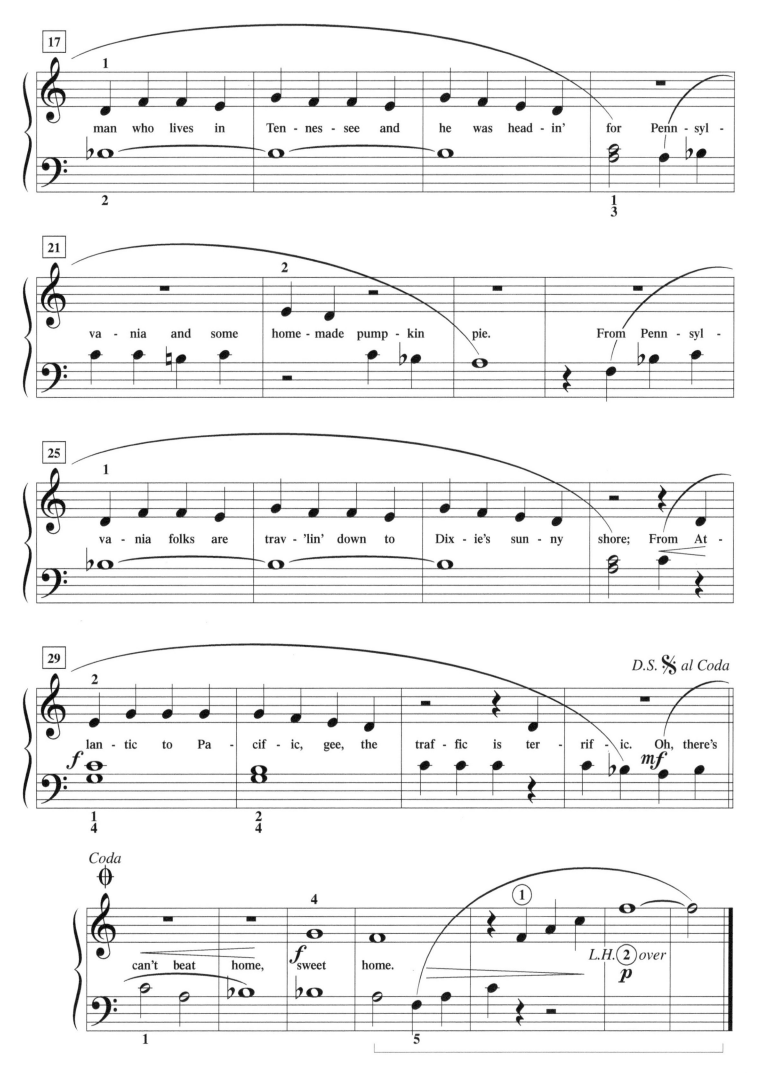

It Came Upon the Midnight Clear

Words by Edmund Hamilton Sears

Music by Richard Storrs Willis

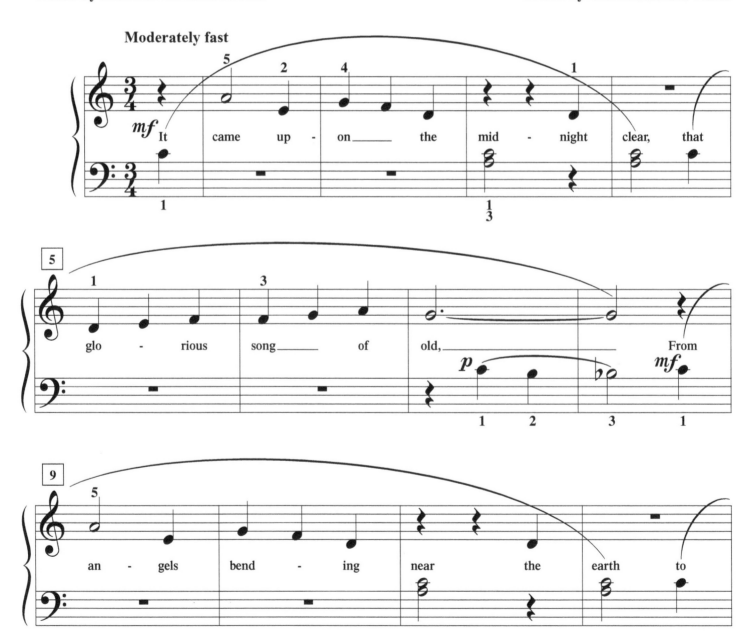

O Little Town of Bethlehem

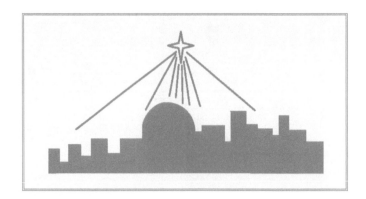

Words by Phillips Brooks

Music by Lewis H. Redner

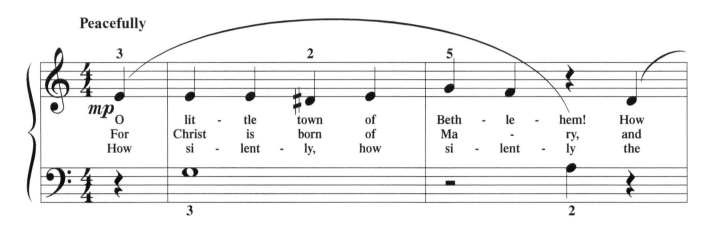

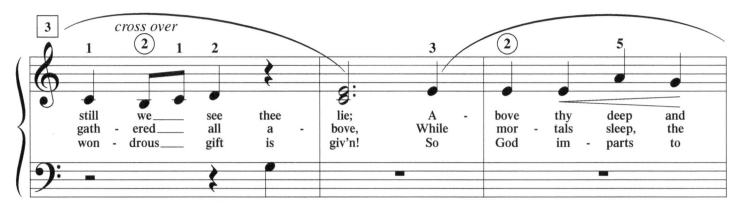

Teacher Duet: (Student plays 1 octave higher)

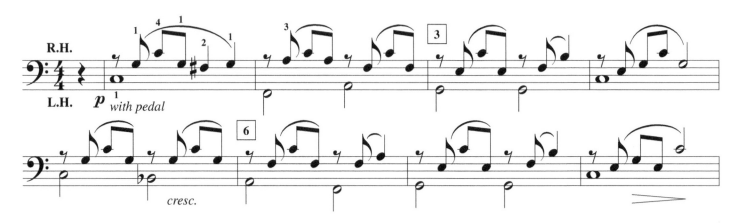

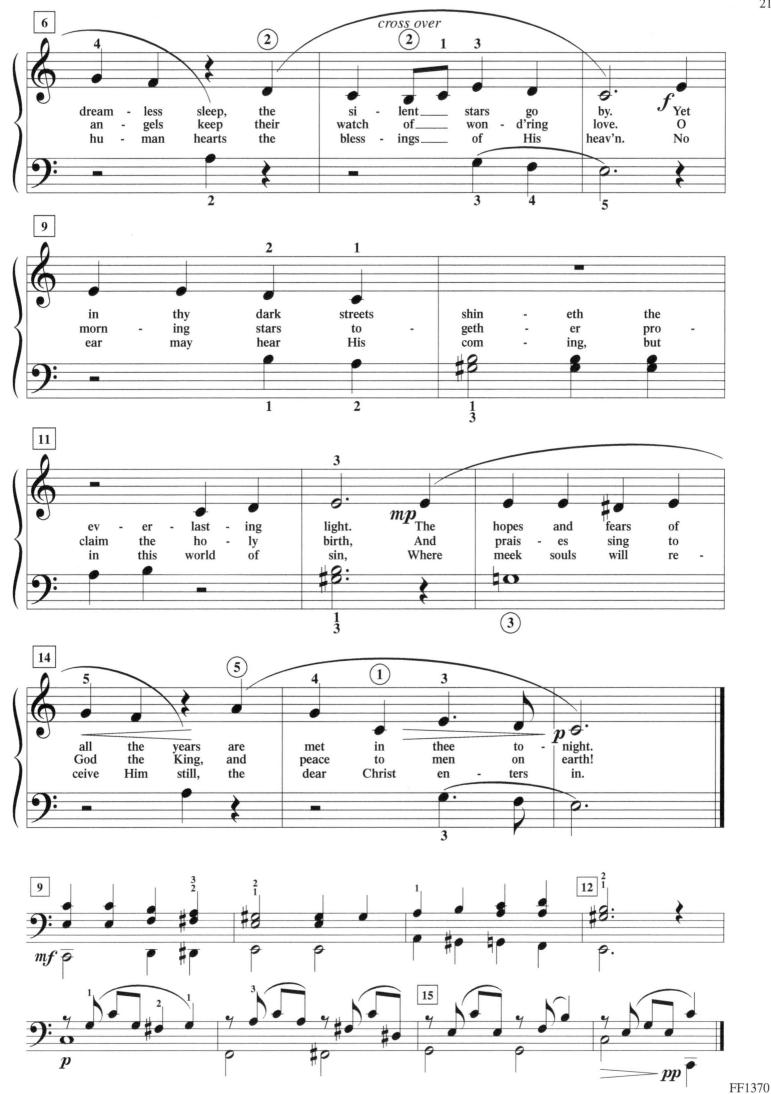

O Come, All Ye Faithful
(Adeste Fideles)

Wade's Cantus Diversi
Transcribed by Frederick Oakeley

Boldly

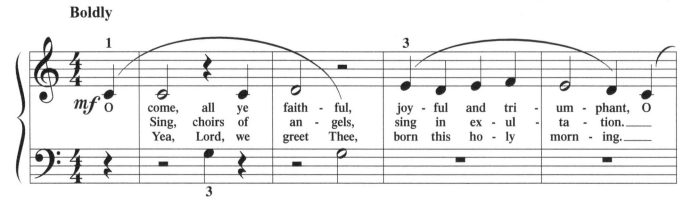

mf O come, all ye faithful, joy - ful and tri - um - phant, O
Sing, choirs of an - gels, sing in ex - ul - ta - tion.___
Yea, Lord, we greet Thee, born this ho - ly morn - ing.___

come ye, O come___ ye to Beth - le - hem.
Sing, all ye cit - i - zens of heav'n___ a - bove!
Je - sus, to Thee___ be___ glo - ry giv'n!

Teacher Duet: (Student plays 1 octave higher)

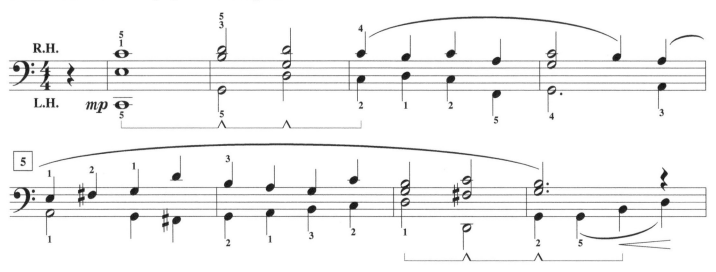

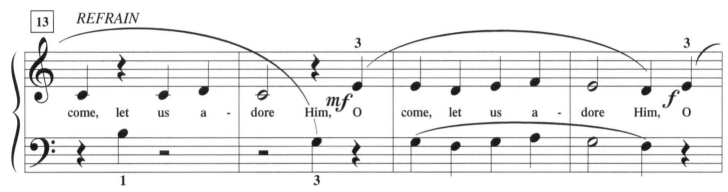

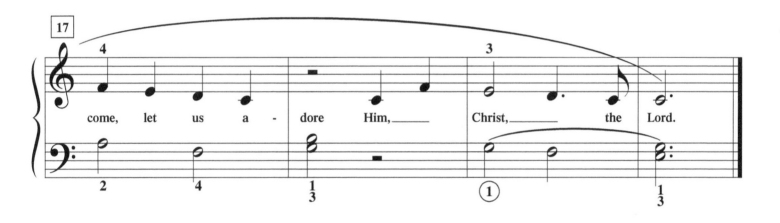

Bring a Torch, Jeannette, Isabella

Traditional

Brightly

Bring a torch,_____ Jean - nette, Is - a - bel - la;
Has - ten now,_____ good folk of the vil - lage;

Bring a torch,_____ come the swift - ly and run.
Has - ten now,_____ the Christ - Child to see.

Christ is born, tell the folk of the vil - lage;
You will find Him a - sleep in the man - ger;

Teacher Duet: (Student plays as written; without pedal)

mf with pedal

Go, Tell It on the Mountain

Traditional

Moderately, with swing

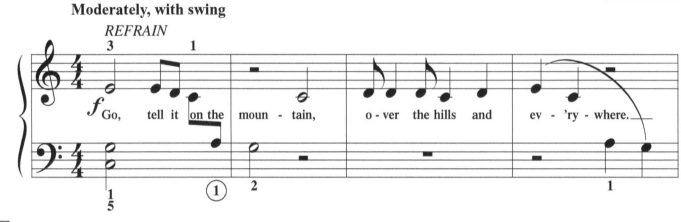

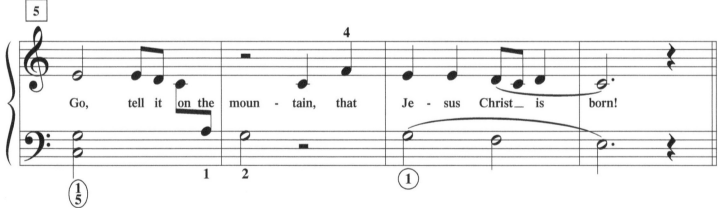

Teacher Duet: (Student plays 1 octave higher)

CHRISTMAS SONGS IN THE KEY OF C MAJOR
(with I, IV, and V7 Chords)

DING, DONG MERRILY ON HIGH (page 36)
Though thoroughly accepted as a traditional Christmas carol, this French tune has its origins in "hedonism and uninhibited enjoyment" (New Oxford Book of Carols). It is a dance from the *Orchésographie*, a 16th century archive of the music and choreography of the day. Although the music is French, it was the English and Irish lyricists Wood and Woodward who turned the dance into one of our most popular Christmas carols.

FROSTY THE SNOWMAN (page 47)
Gene Autry, the "Singing Cowboy," introduced *Frosty the Snowman* to the world with his 1951 recording of the Steve Nelson's and Jack Rollins's song. *Frosty* quickly rose through the charts to become a million seller, and continues to bring Christmas cheer to children.

GOOD KING WENCESLAS (page 31)
The titled is a misnomer because Wenceslas was not a king, but the Duke of Bohemia. Wenceslas was a good and honest man who was martyred after being murdered by his jealous younger brother. In 1853 John M. Neale selected the noble Wenceslas as the lyrical inspiration for this children's tune, which illustrates the virtue of generosity. The music is a spring carol that first appeared in 1582 in a collection of Swedish church and school songs.

I'LL BE HOME FOR CHRISTMAS (page 54)
Bing Crosby recorded *I'll Be Home for Christmas* midway through the dark days of World War II. The song reflects not only the melancholy feelings of servicemen and their families during time of war, but the longing and hope of all those separated from their families at Christmas.

JINGLE-BELL ROCK (page 44)
Ad-man Joe Beal and writer Jim Boothe were not paying homage to the Christmas classic *Jingle Bells* when they wrote their popular song *Jingle–Bell Rock* in 1957. Rather, they were capitalizing on the popularity of the then-new musical form "rock 'n' roll" to create a novelty song with a contemporary feel.

JOY TO THE WORLD (page 34)

The words, based on verses from Psalm 98 in the Old Testament, pre-date the accompaniment by almost 120 years. American composer and music educator Lowell Mason set the text to music, creating several different arrangements which he modestly attributed to George Frideric Handel. Handel's involvement was accepted until musicologists proved that no portion of the music came straight from any of Handel's compositions.

(ALL I WANT FOR CHRISTMAS IS) MY TWO FRONT TEETH (page 52)

Novelty songs have been popular at Christmas for at least the past 70 years. *All I Want for Christmas Is My Two Front Teeth* was introduced on Perry Como's radio show and subsequently was a 1948 hit for Spike Jones & His City Slickers.

O CHRISTMAS TREE (page 50)

The custom of decorating Christmas trees arose in Germany around the same time as Ernst Anschütz wrote this carol (1824). Anschütz took the melody from a song titled "Es lebe doch," which was first published in 1799. *O Tannenbaum* (O Christmas Tree) became the most popular carol about the Christmas tree. Tannenbaum is literally translated as "fir tree."

SANTA CLAUS IS COMIN' TO TOWN (page 38)

The caution "you better watch out, you better not cry, you better not pout" and the promise of "Santa Claus is coming to town" have captured the imaginations of children since the Great Depression, when the song was written. Although it has become the third-best-selling Christmas song of all time, behind *White Christmas* and *Rudolph the Red-Nosed Reindeer*, music publishers had turned it down for being noncommercial. That is, until it was performed on Eddie Cantor's radio show. And the rest, as they say, is history.

SILENT NIGHT (page 32)

There's a saying that necessity is the mother of invention, and when the pipe organ gave out in priest Joseph Mohr's Catholic church on Christmas Eve, 1818, church organist Franz Grüber improvised, creating a simple tune for a tenor, bass and two guitars. The combination of Mohr's holiday verses with Grüber's gentle melody yielded "Silent Night," which went on to become one of the most popular pieces of Christmas music.

THE TWELVE DAYS OF CHRISTMAS (page 40)

This traditional song dates back to the 16th century, when counting songs were very much in vogue. At the time, the practice was to try to extend holidays as long as possible, and Christmas was celebrated for twelve days, from Christmas day to the Epiphany. The appeal of this carol was that even if you couldn't afford to give gifts for twelve consecutive days, you could at least sing about them.

KEY OF C

C Major Scale

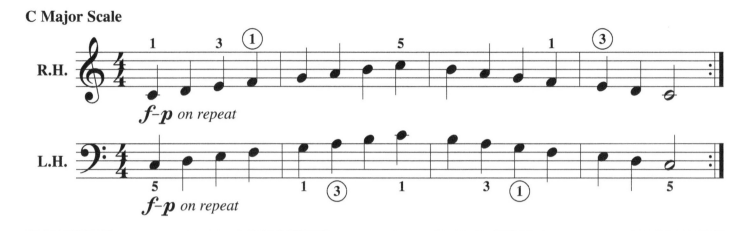

R.H.

f-p on repeat

L.H.

f-p on repeat

Primary Chords

The **I**, **IV**, and **V** chords are called the *primary* chords.
They are built on scale degrees 1, 4, and 5 of the major scale.

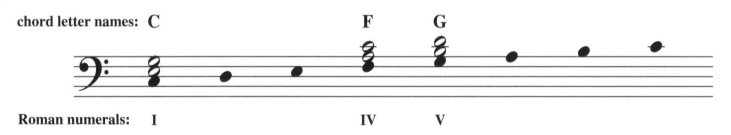

chord letter names: C   F   G

Roman numerals: I   IV   V

C, **F**, and **G** are the **I**, **IV**, and **V** chords in the Key of C.

Common Chord Positions

The chords above are shown in the *root position*, built up in 3rds from the chord *root* (chord name).
By inverting the notes, the **I**, **IV**, and **V7** chords can be played with little motion of the hand.

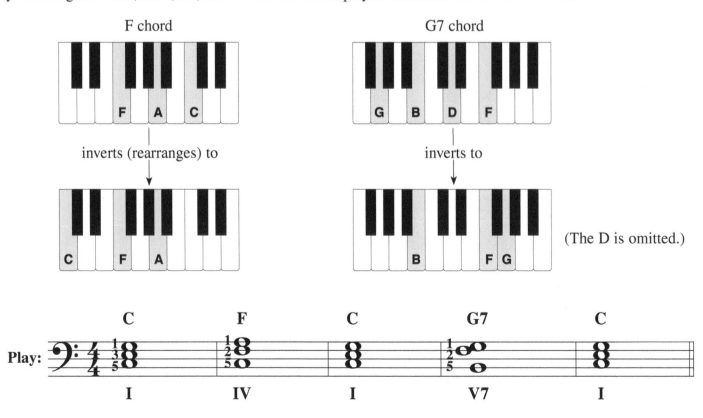

F chord

G7 chord

inverts (rearranges) to

inverts to

(The D is omitted.)

Play:

C   F   C   G7   C

I   IV   I   V7   I

Good King Wenceslas

Traditional

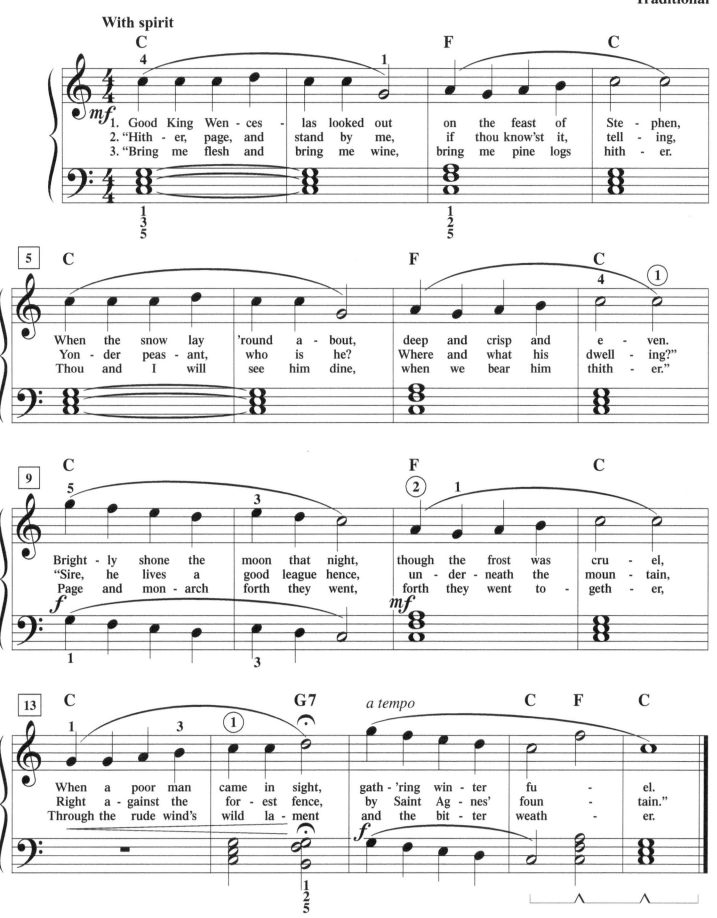

Silent Night

Words by Joseph Mohr

Music by Franz Grüber

Slowly, peacefully

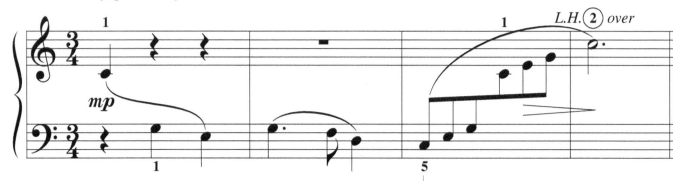

1. Si - lent night, ho - ly night,
2. Si - lent night, ho - ly night,
3. Si - lent night, ho - ly night,

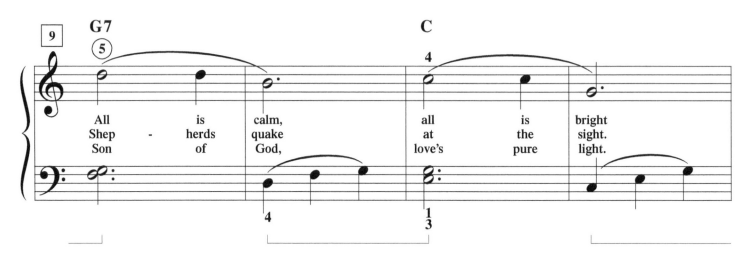

All is calm, all is bright sight.
Shep - herds quake at the pure sight.
Son of God, love's pure light.

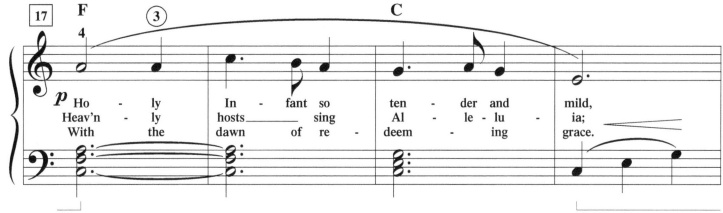

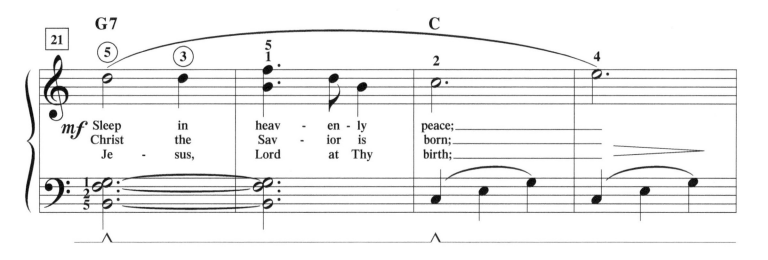

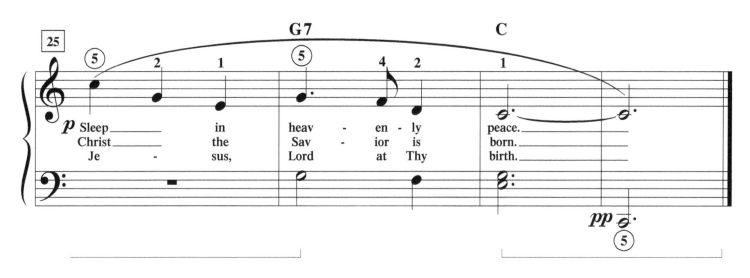

Joy to the World

Words by Isaac Watts

Music by Lowell Mason
(commonly attributed to G. F. Handel)

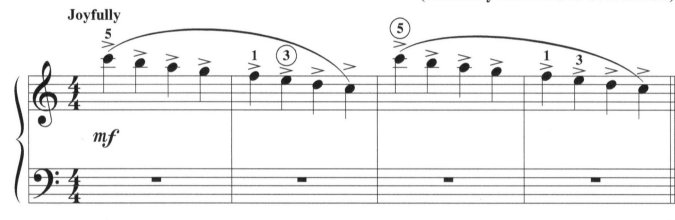

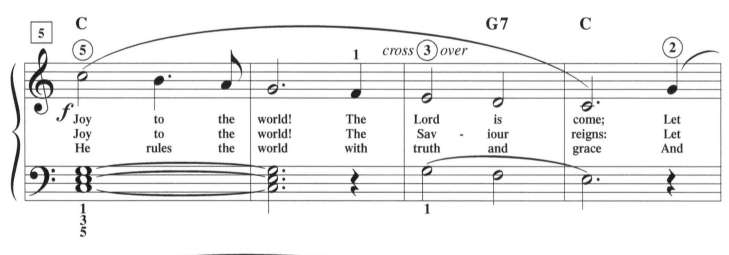

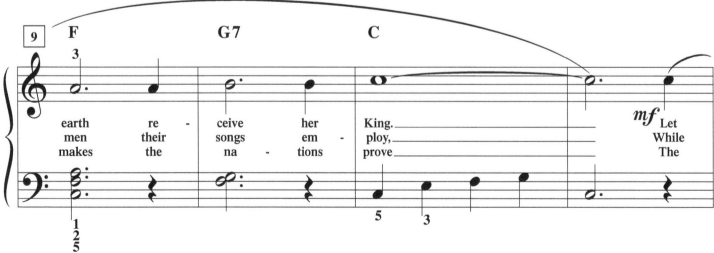

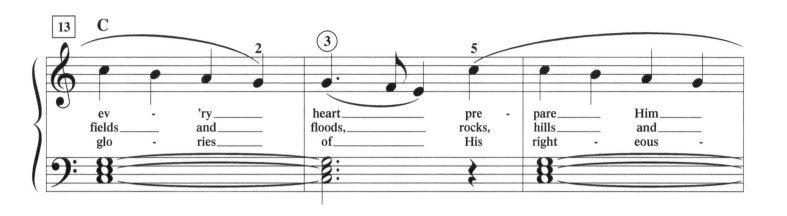

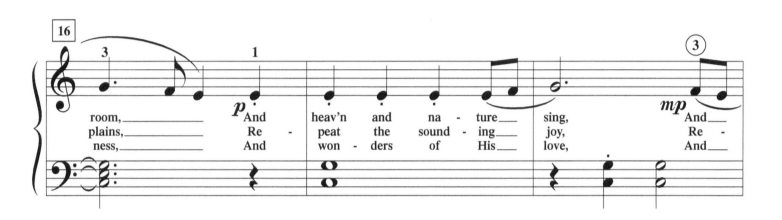

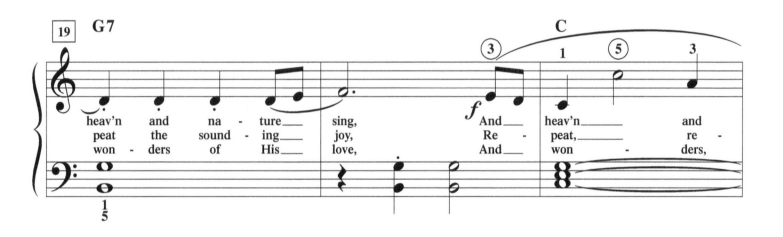

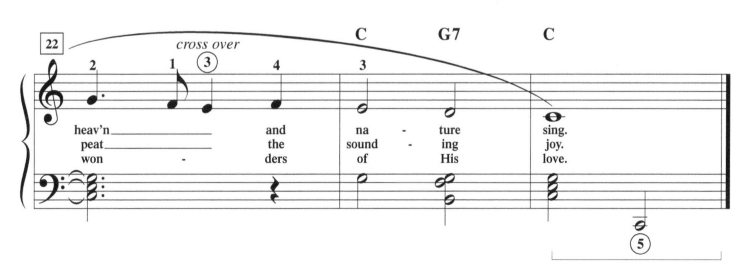

Ding, Dong Merrily on High

French Dance

Joyfully

Ding, dong, mer - ri - ly on high, the Christ - mas bells are

ring - ing. Ding, dong, joy - ous - ly re - ply, the

an - gels all a - sing - ing. Glo -

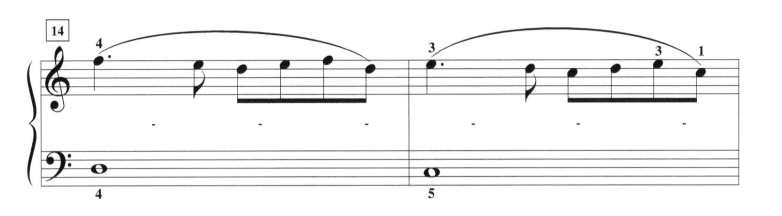

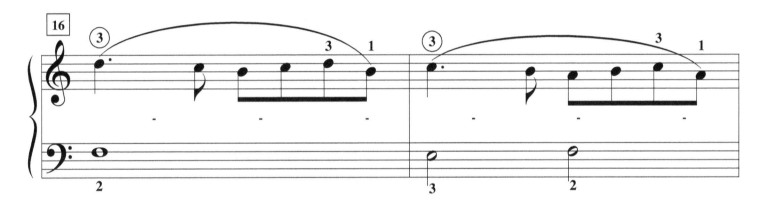

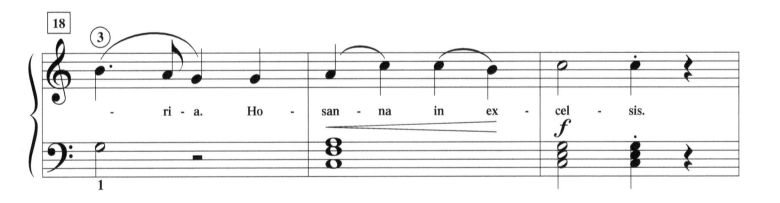

- ri - a. Ho - san - na in ex - cel - sis.

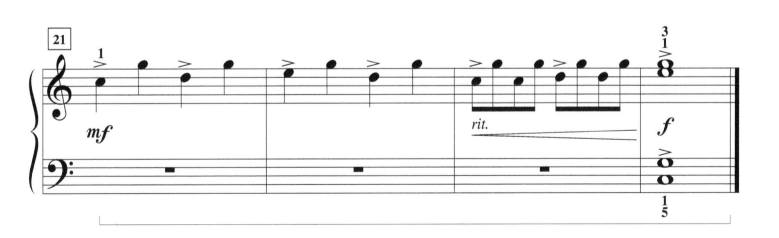

Santa Claus Is Comin' to Town

Words by Haven Gillespie   **Music by J. Fred Coots**

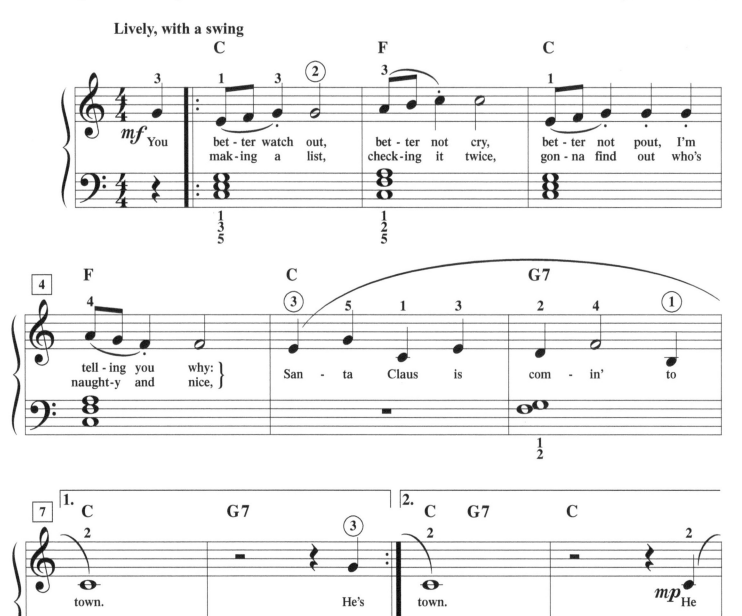

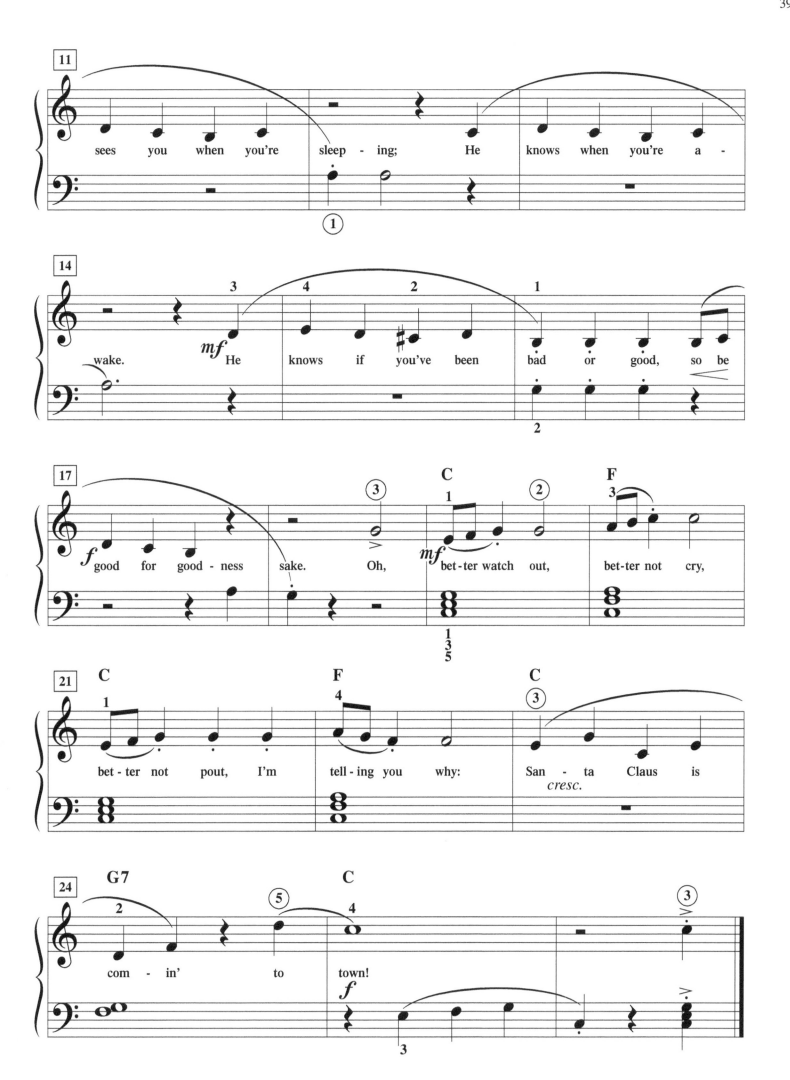

The Twelve Days of Christmas

Traditional

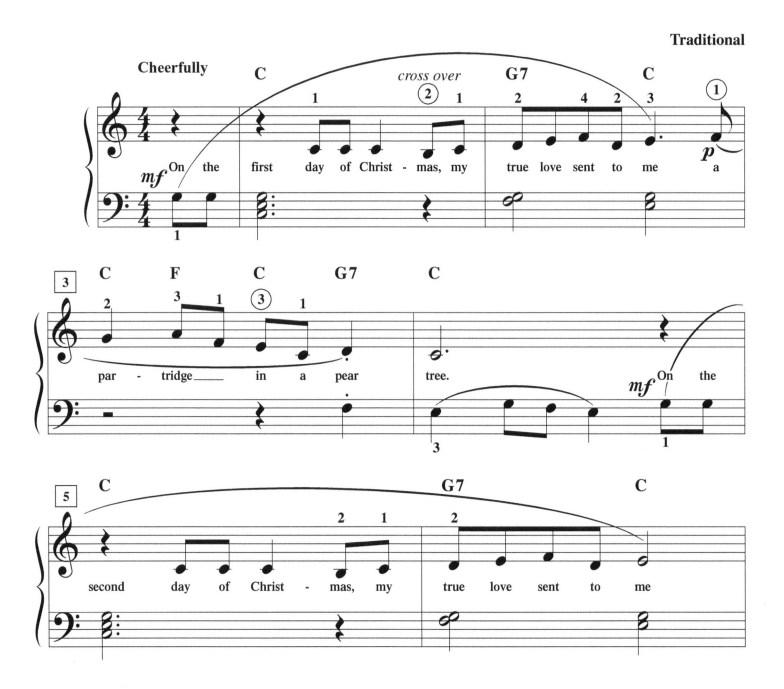

42

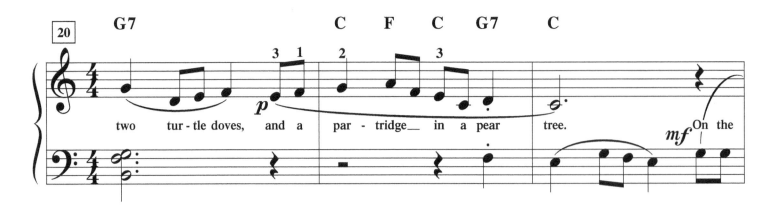

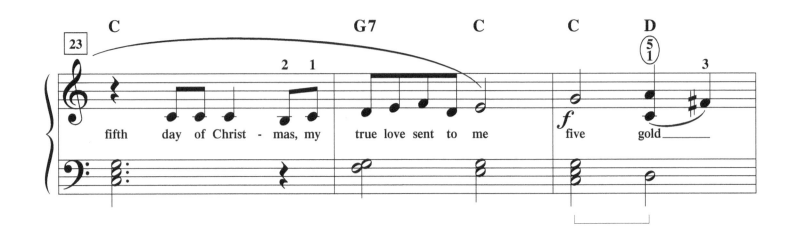

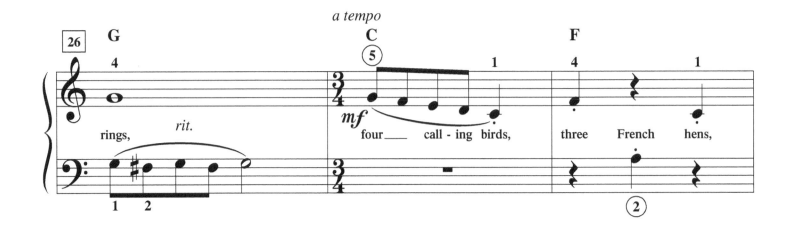

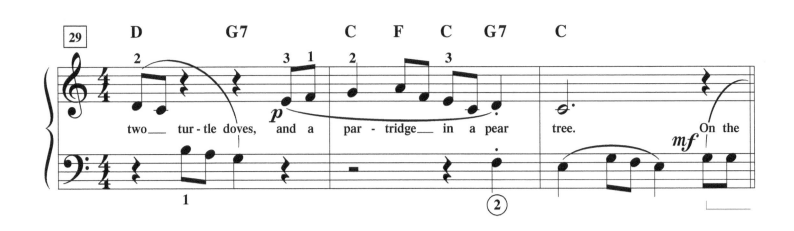

43

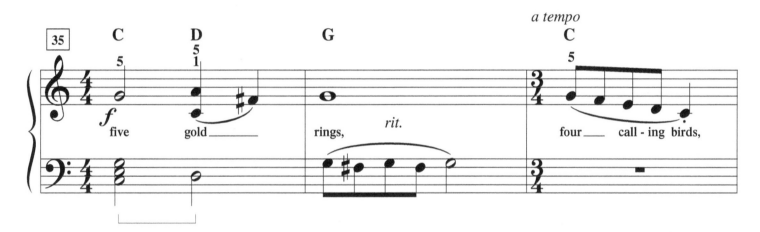

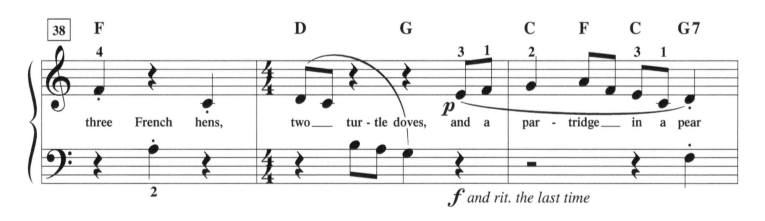

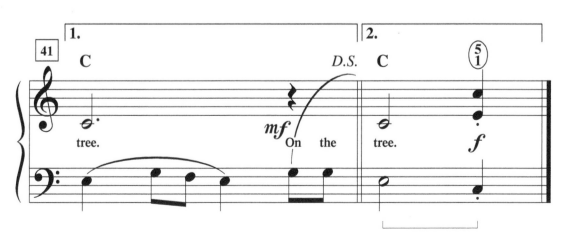

FF1370

Jingle-Bell Rock

**Words and Music by
Joe Beal and Jim Boothe**

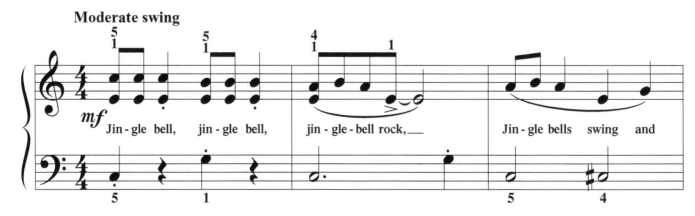

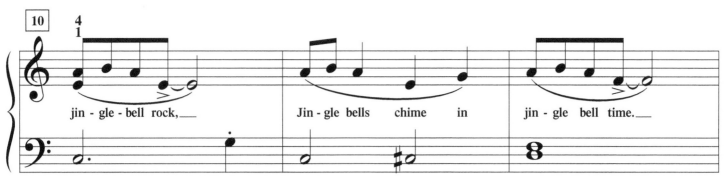

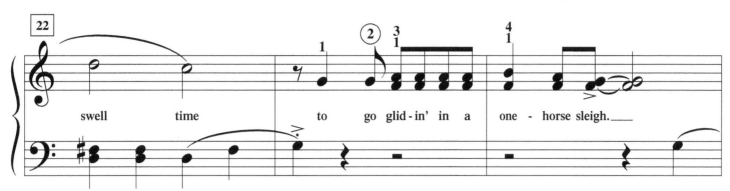

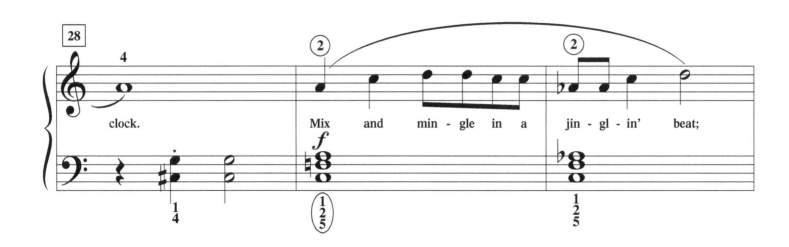

34 **Slower (no swing)**

Frosty the Snowman

**Words and Music by
Steve Nelson and Jack Rollins**

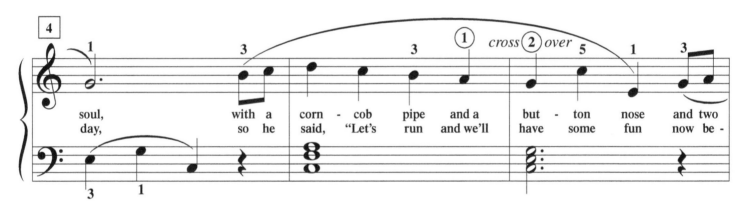

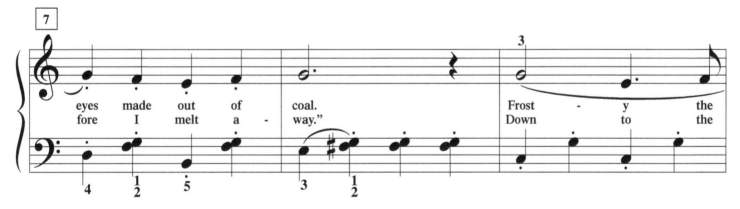

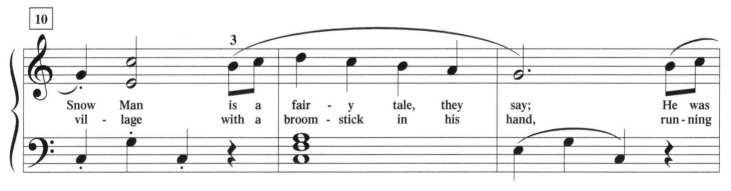

FF1370

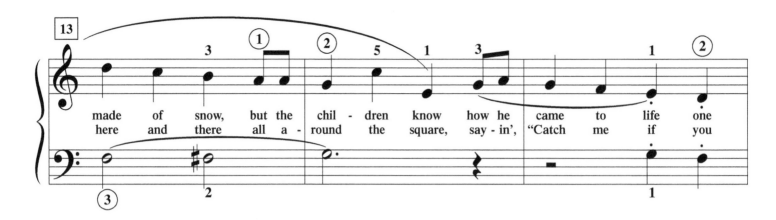

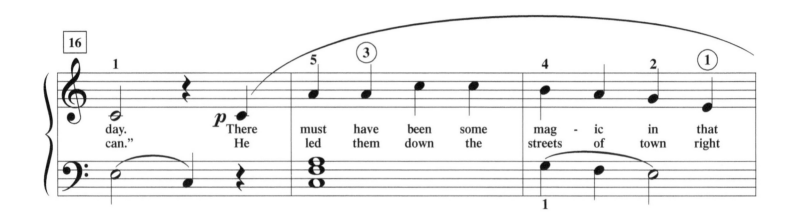

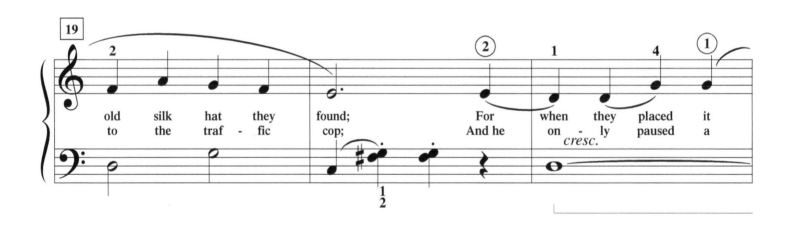

O *Christmas Tree*

(O Tannenbaum)

Traditional

Majestically

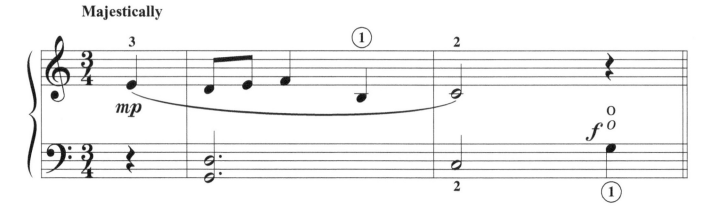

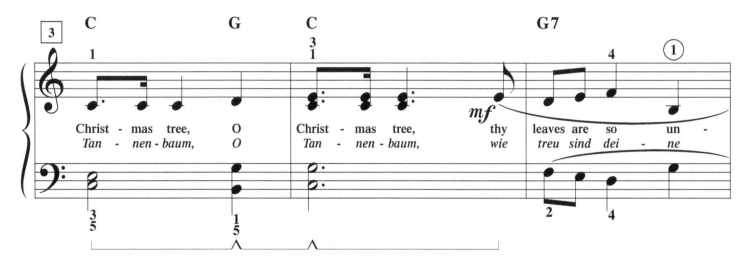

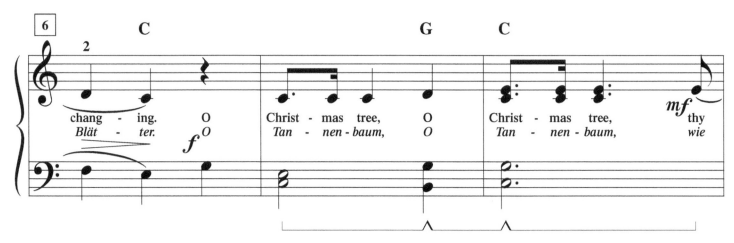

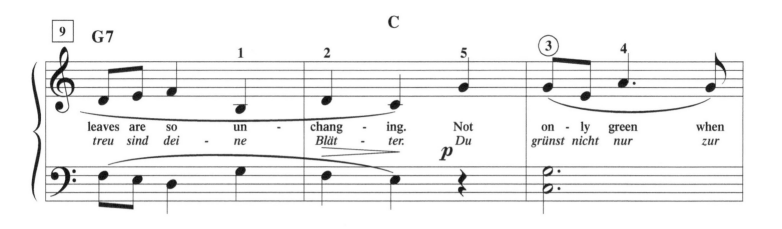

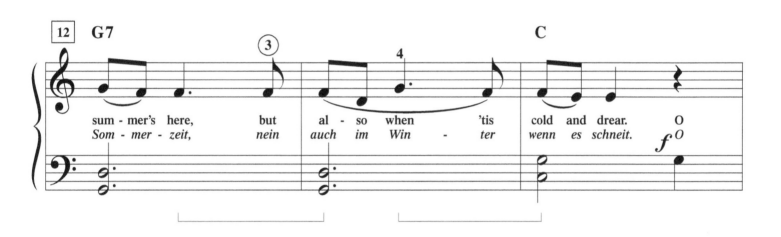

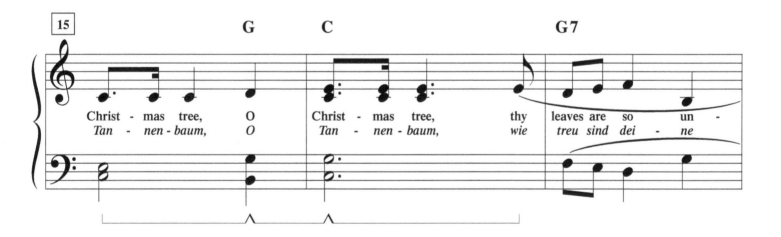

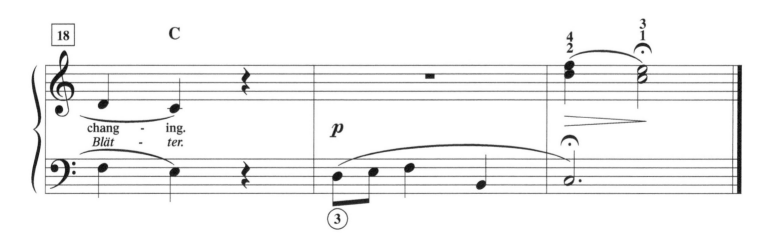

(All I Want for Christmas Is)
My Two Front Teeth

**Words and Music by
Don Gardner**

Moderately

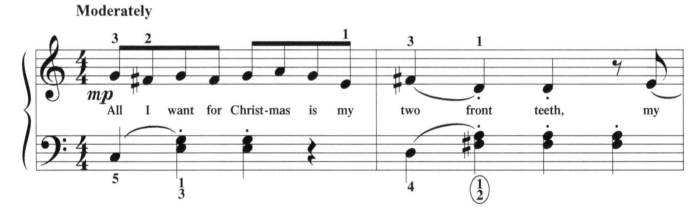

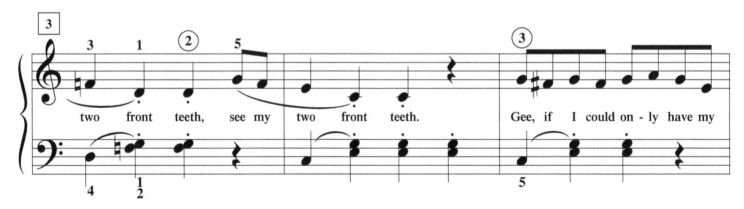

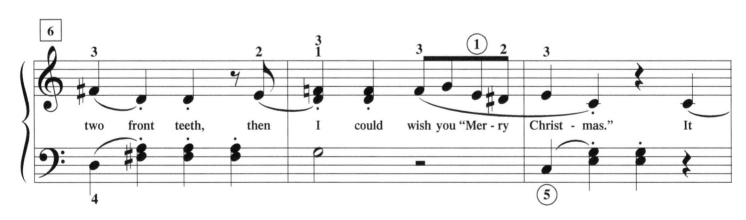

I'll Be Home for Christmas

Words by Kim Gannon

Music by Walter Kent

CHRISTMAS SONGS IN THE KEY OF G MAJOR
(with I, IV, and V7 Chords)

AULD LANG SYNE (page 76)

The Scottish tune that has become synonymous with New Year's Eve (the title's literal translation is "old long ago") is perfectly suited for closing the old year and bringing in the new. Though the composer of the melody is unknown, the lyric is credited to Robert Burns, an 18th century poet who adapted the words from traditional Scottish songs.

BLUE CHRISTMAS (page 72)

Although first a hit in 1948 for Ernest Tubb, Elvis Presley made the Billy Hayes and Jay Johnson song his own. Like *I'll Be Home for Christmas* before it, *Blue Christmas* reflects the melancholy that can accompany a joyful season.

DECK THE HALL (page 59)

This Welsh folk tune originated as a song for folk dancing and Irish harp. The participants would encircle the harpist and sing a line of verse. Then the harpist would answer instrumentally with the melody that is now "Fa la la la la . . ." Eventually, the original tune became known as *New Year's Eve*.

THE FIRST NOEL (page 62)

Carols date back almost to the Nativity. In the 2nd century the bishop of Rome initiated the singing of carols to celebrate Christmas. This 17th century carol, or ring dance, comes from either England or France—the exact source is uncertain. At that time one couldn't sing in church, even at Christmas. So, the congregation sang outside after services. People frequently made up new verses, which accounts for differences between the text of the song and that of the scriptures, such as shepherds seeing the star.

HARK! THE HERALD ANGELS SING (page 68)

Many of Charles Wesley's 6,000 hymn texts were adopted by the Methodist church, which was founded by his brother John. The lyric "Hark, how all the heaven rings," was revised by his friend George Whitfield to the line we sing today. It was 100 years later though, in 1855, that English organist W.H. Cummings adapted and applied the text to festive music from a Felix Mendelssohn cantata. The marriage of Wesley's lyric and Mendelssohn's chorus struck a joyous chord, and soon became a Christmas classic.

HAVE YOURSELF A MERRY LITTLE CHRISTMAS (page 74)

Judy Garland first performed this upbeat Christmas tune in the 1944 film *Meet Me in St. Louis*, just five years after she played Dorothy in *The Wizard of Oz*. However, Ms. Garland felt that the original lyrics were too pessimistic for the dark days of World War II, and she asked that words be written that would be more hopeful.

I SAW THREE SHIPS (page 60)

First published in 1666, the melody and lyric have folk origins in the British Isles. The sea trading activity of the region undoubtedly influenced the lyric, as did the story about the remains of the three Wise Men being carried by ship to Europe. The ships are sailing to Bethlehem on Christmas morning. Some interpret the three ships figuratively—symbolic of the Trinity, or the Virgin mother and Christ child.

THE LITTLE DRUMMER BOY (page 64)

Harry Simeone wrote and the Harry Simeone Chorale sang this relatively recent Christmas classic about a poor shepherd boy who followed the Star of Bethlehem to the manger and gave the baby Jesus all he had to give—his drum and his song.

SUZY SNOWFLAKE (page 70)

The well-known songwriting team of Tepper and Bennett wrote *Suzy Snowflake* for Tepper's newborn daughter Susan. It proved to be one of the writing team's most beloved songs, along with their hits *Red Roses for a Blue Lady* and *The Naughty Lady of Shady Lane*.

TREPAK (FROM THE NUTCRACKER SUITE) (page 66)

Trepak—a fast and lively Russian dance—is from Tchaikovsky's famous third ballet. It's based on a story by E.T.A. Hoffmann about a young girl who dreams of her favorite Christmas gift, a nutcracker. The ballet was an instant hit upon its debut in 1892.

58

KEY OF G

G Major Scale

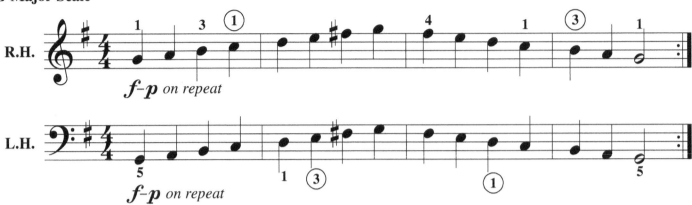

f-p *on repeat*

f-p *on repeat*

Primary Chords in G

REVIEW: The primary chords are built on scale degrees 1, 4, and 5 of the major scale.
NEW: Here are the **I**, **IV**, and **V** chords in the Key of G.

chord letter names: G   C   D

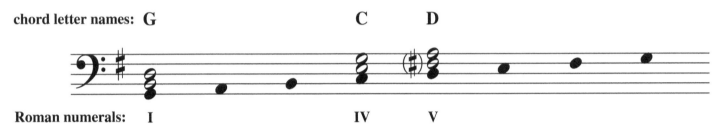

Roman numerals: I   IV   V

In the Key of G the **I**, **IV**, and **V** chords are **G**, **C**, and **D**.

Common Chord Positions

By inverting the notes, the **I**, **IV**, and **V7** chords can be played with little motion of the hand.

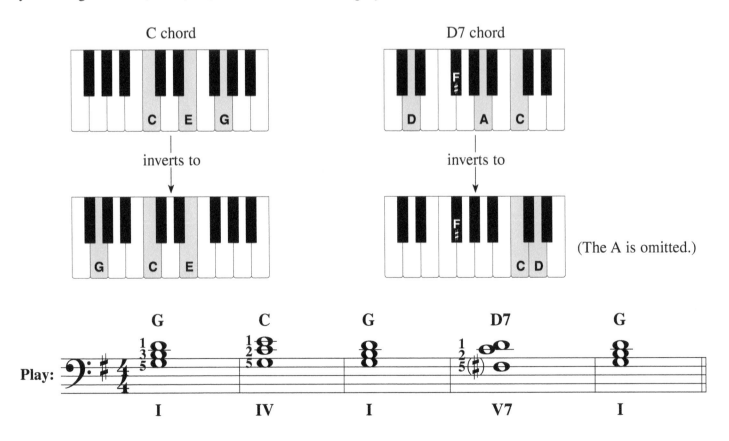

FF1370

Deck the Hall

Traditional

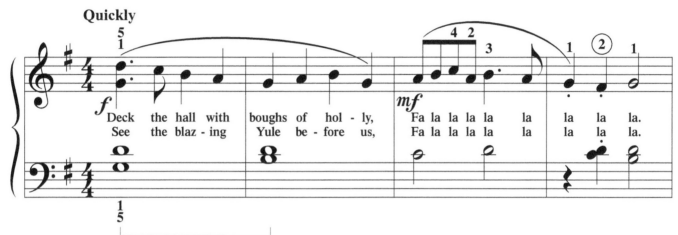

Deck the hall with boughs of hol - ly,
Fa la la la la la la la la.
See the blaz - ing Yule be - fore us,
Fa la la la la la la la la.

'Tis the sea - son to be jol - ly,
Fa la la la la la la la la.
Strike the harp and join the cho - rus,
Fa la la la la la la la la.

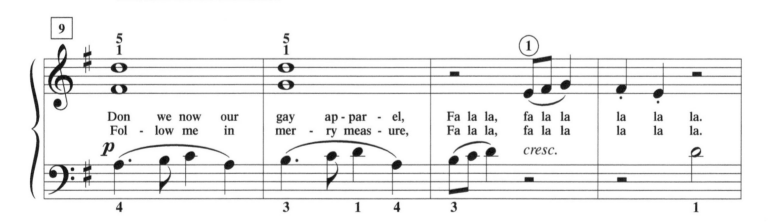

Don we now our gay ap - par - el,
Fa la la, fa la la la la la.
Fol - low me in mer - ry meas - ure,
Fa la la, fa la la la la la.

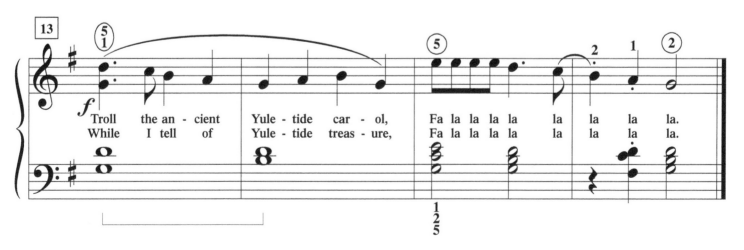

Troll the an - cient Yule - tide car - ol,
Fa la la la la la la la la.
While I tell of Yule - tide treas - ure,
Fa la la la la la la la la.

I Saw Three Ships

Traditional

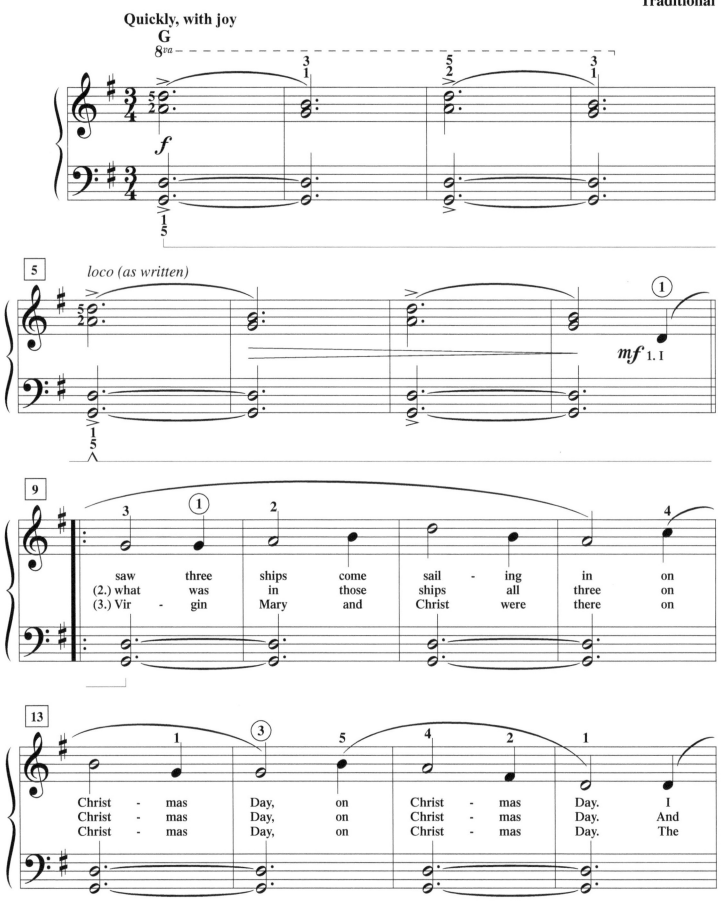

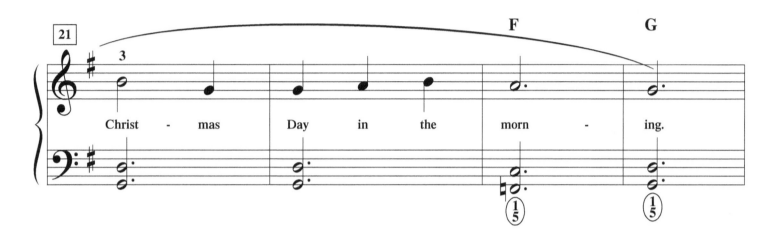

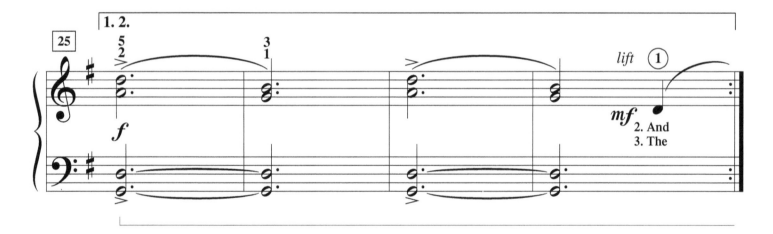

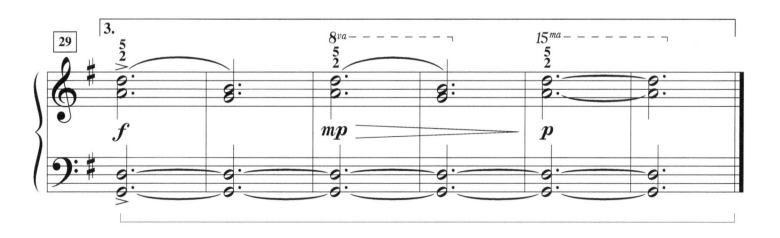

The First Noel

Traditional

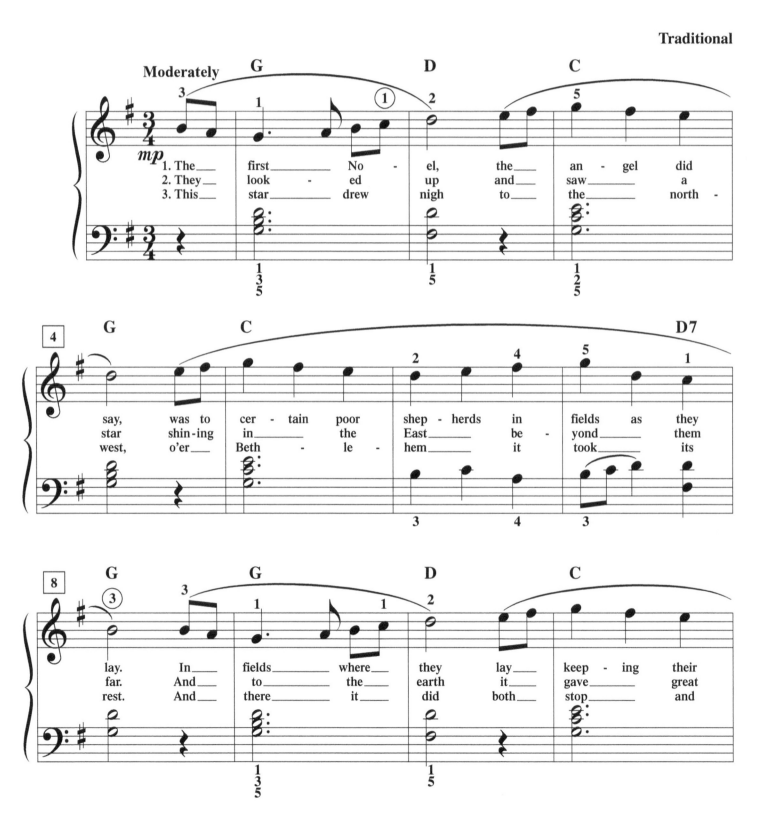

1. The first Noel, the an-gel did say, was to cer-tain poor shep-herds in fields as they lay. In fields where they lay keep-ing their
2. They look-ed up and saw a star shin-ing in the East be-yond them far. And to the earth it gave great
3. This star drew nigh to the north-west, o'er Beth-le-hem it took its rest. And there it did both stop and

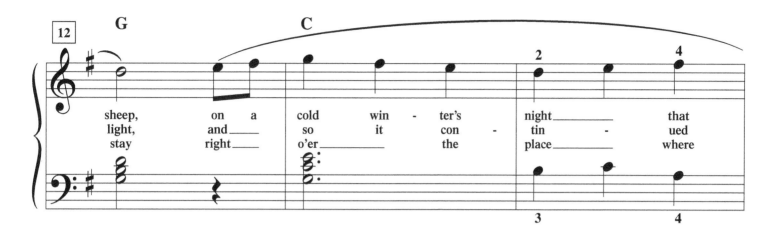

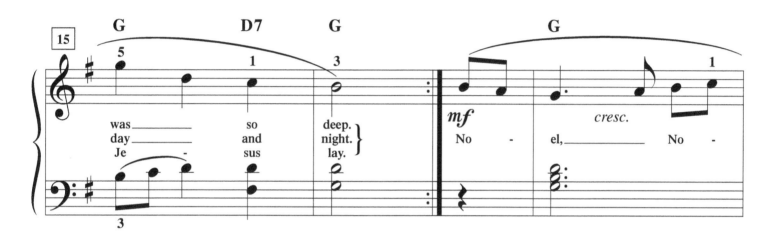

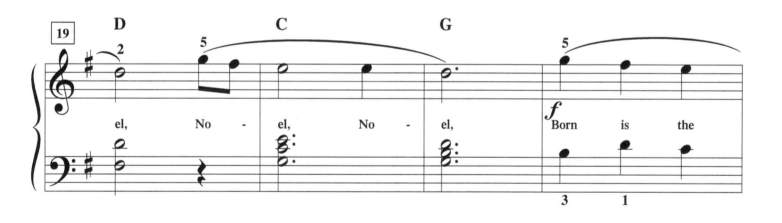

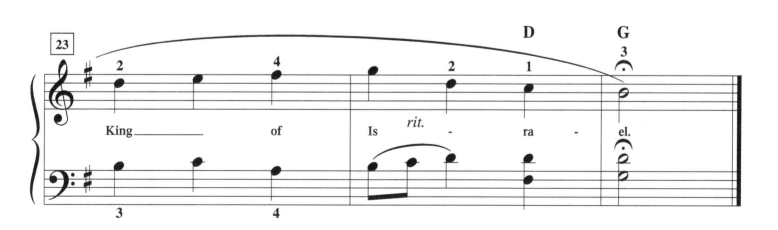

The Little Drummer Boy

**Words and Music by
Katherine Davis, Henry Onorati,
and Harry Simeone**

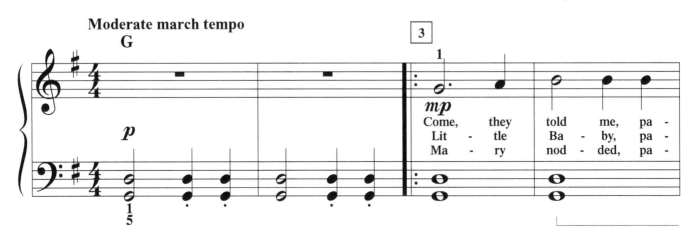

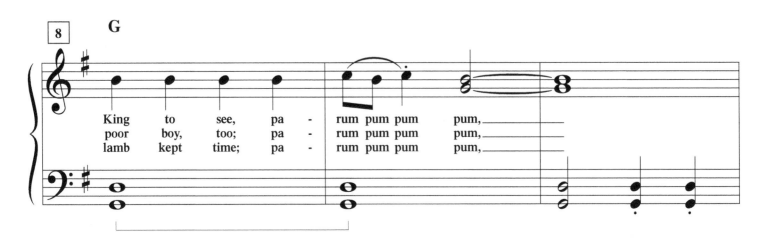

Trepak
from *The Nutcracker Suite*

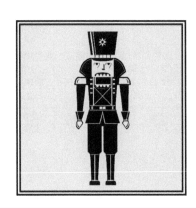

Peter Ilyich Tchaikovsky

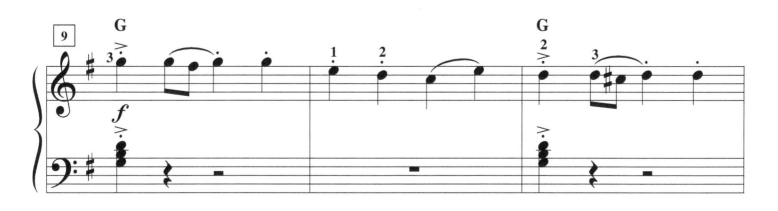

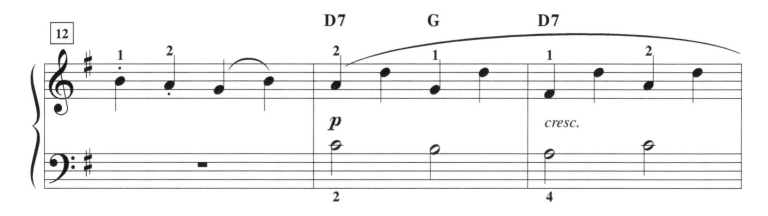

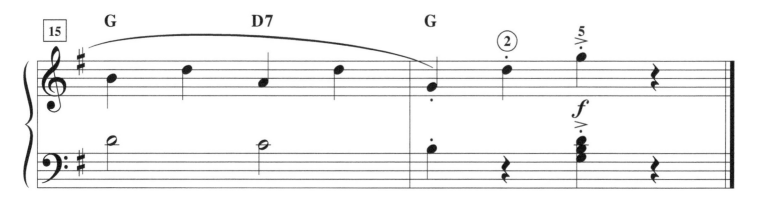

Hark!
The Herald Angels Sing

**By Felix Mendelssohn
and Charles Wesley**

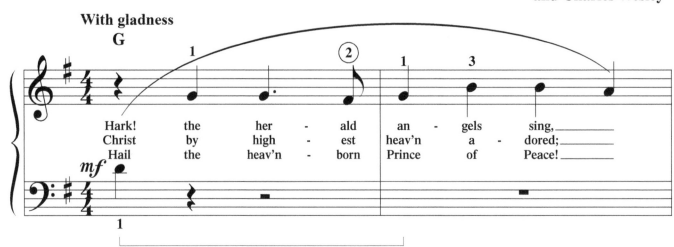

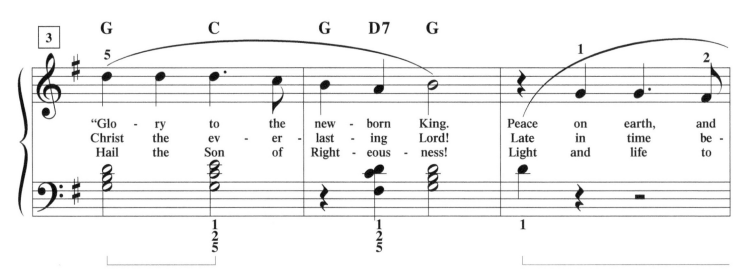

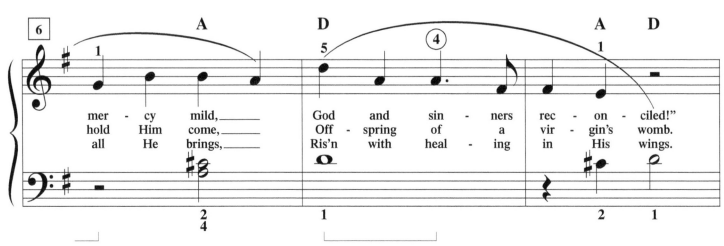

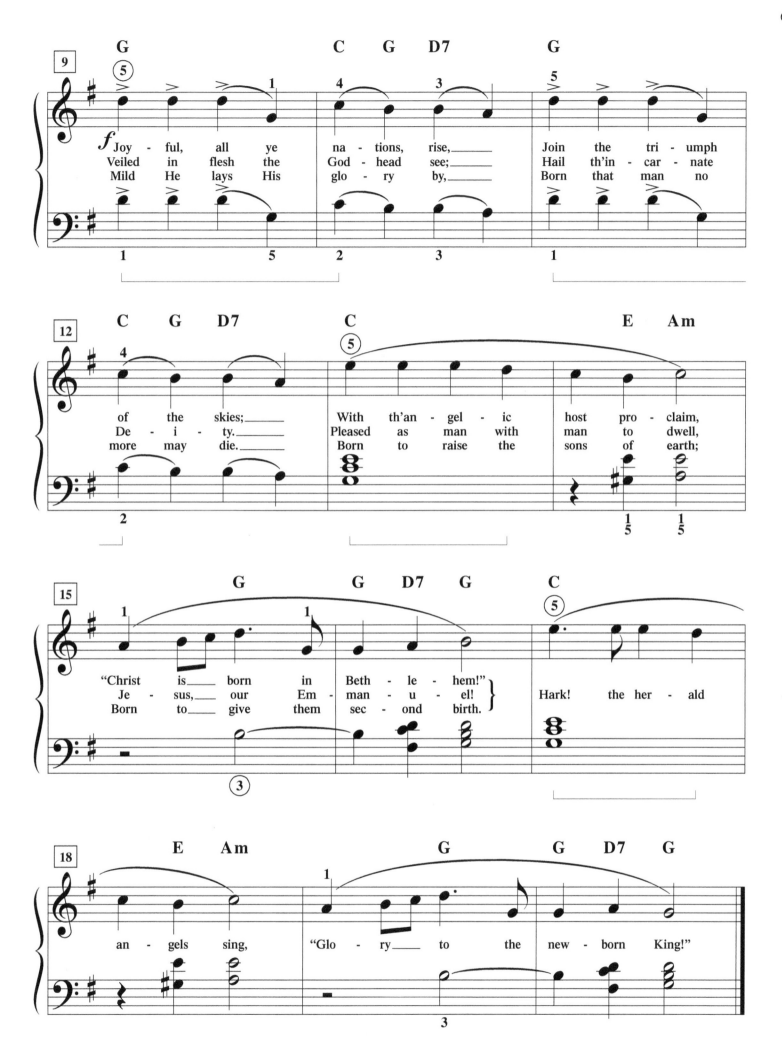

Suzy Snowflake

**Words and Music by
Sid Tepper and Roy C. Bennett**

Moderately, with a swing

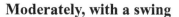

Here comes Su - zy Snow - flake, dressed in a snow - white
Here comes Su - zy snow - flake; soon you will hear her

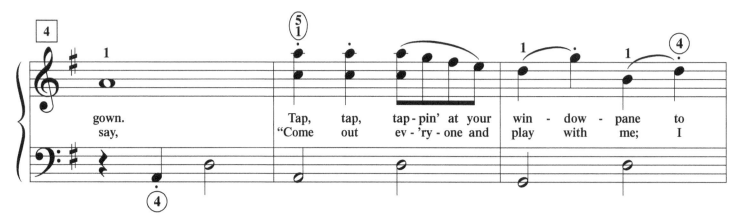

gown.
say,

Tap, tap, tap - pin' at your win - dow - pane to
"Come out ev - 'ry - one and play with me; I

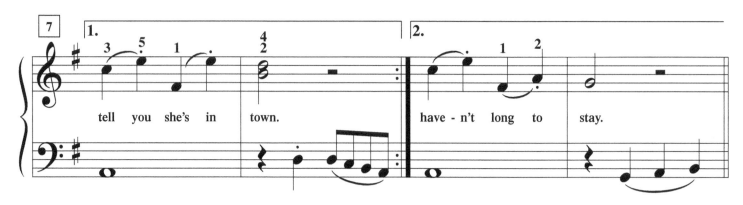

1.
tell you she's in town.

2.
have - n't long to stay.

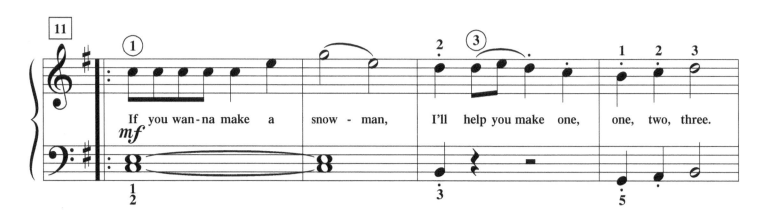

If you wan - na make a snow - man, I'll help you make one, one, two, three.

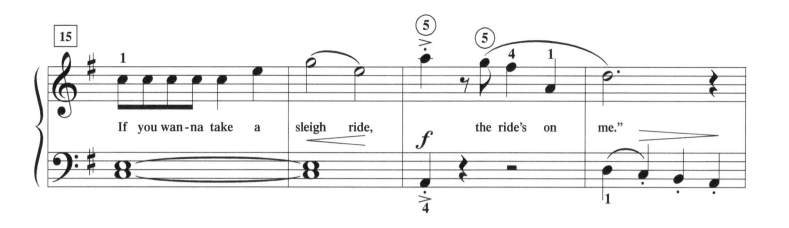

If you wan-na take a sleigh ride, the ride's on me."

Here comes Su - zy Snow-flake; look at her tum - blin' down.

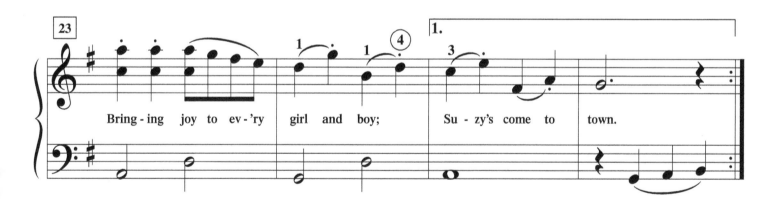

Bring-ing joy to ev-'ry girl and boy; Su - zy's come to town.

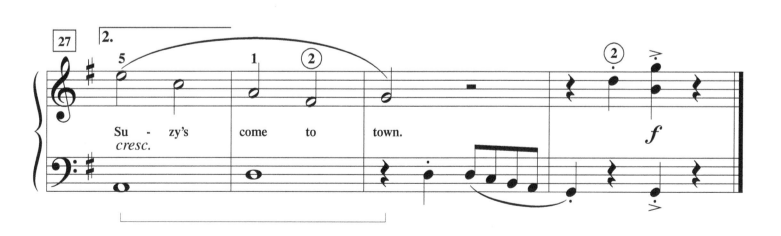

Su - zy's come to town.

Blue Christmas

**Words and Music by
Bill Hayes and Jay Johnson**

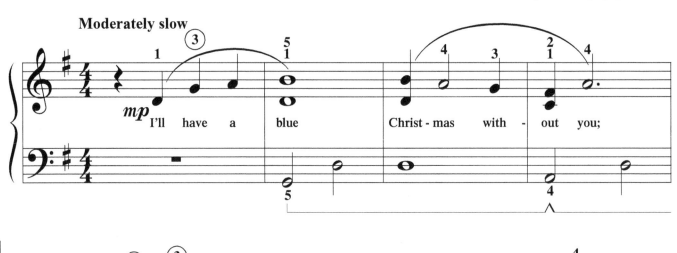

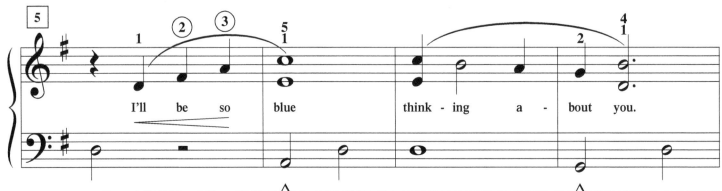

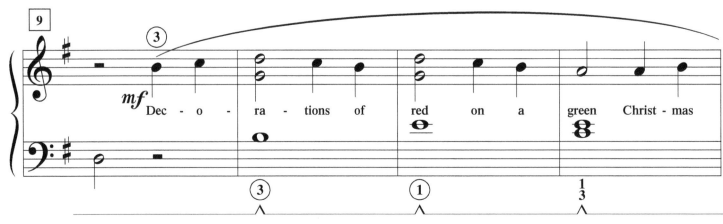

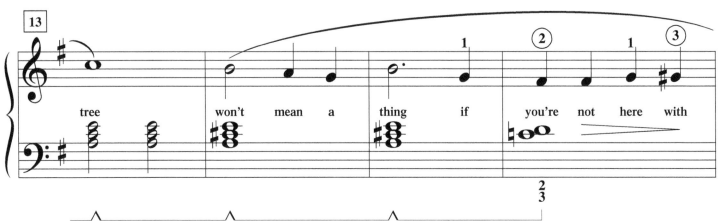

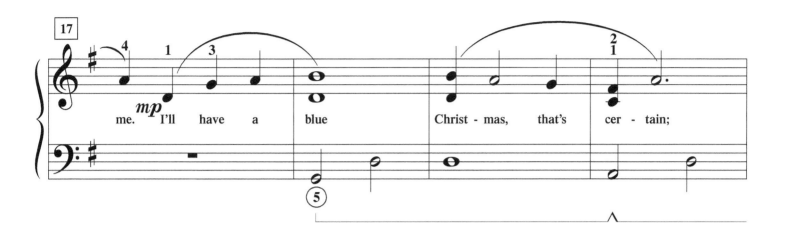

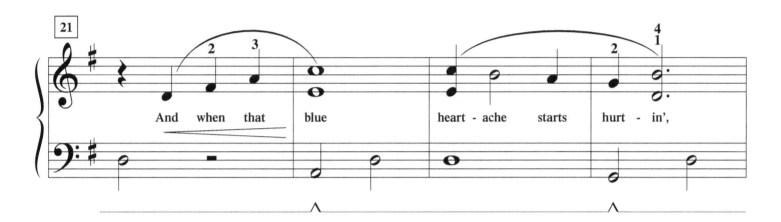

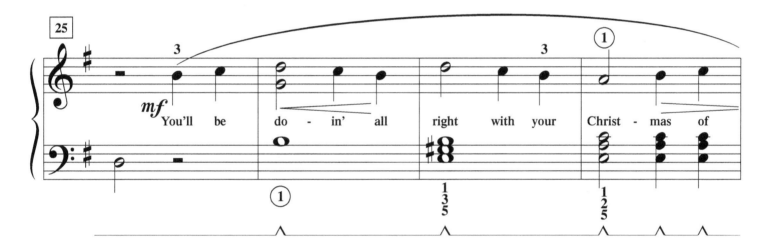

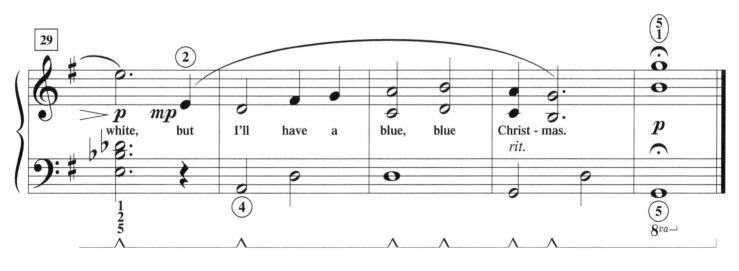

Have Yourself a
Merry Little Christmas

Words and Music by
Hugh Martin and Ralph Blane

Auld Lang Syne

Traditional

Slowly, with expression

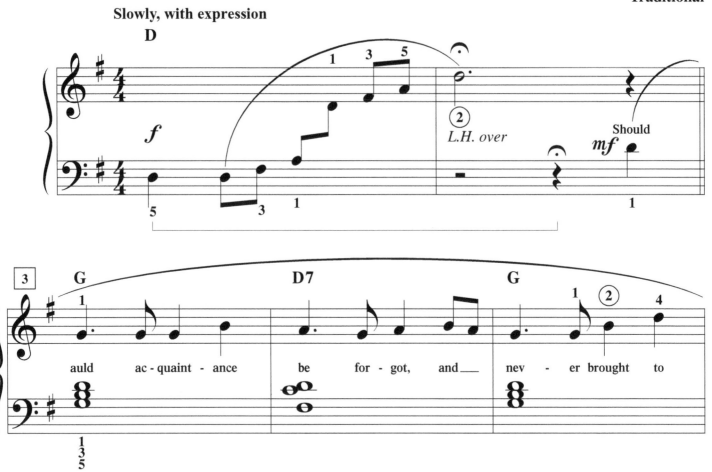

Teacher Duet: (Student plays as written)

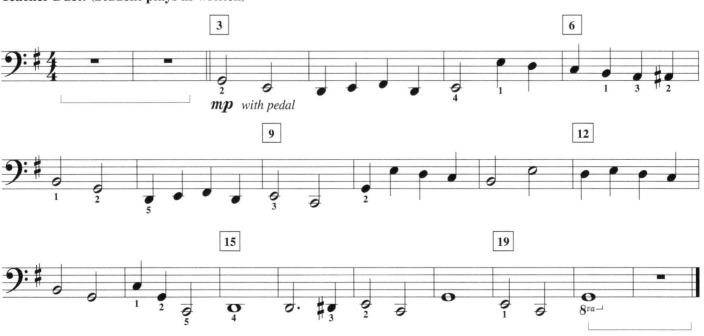

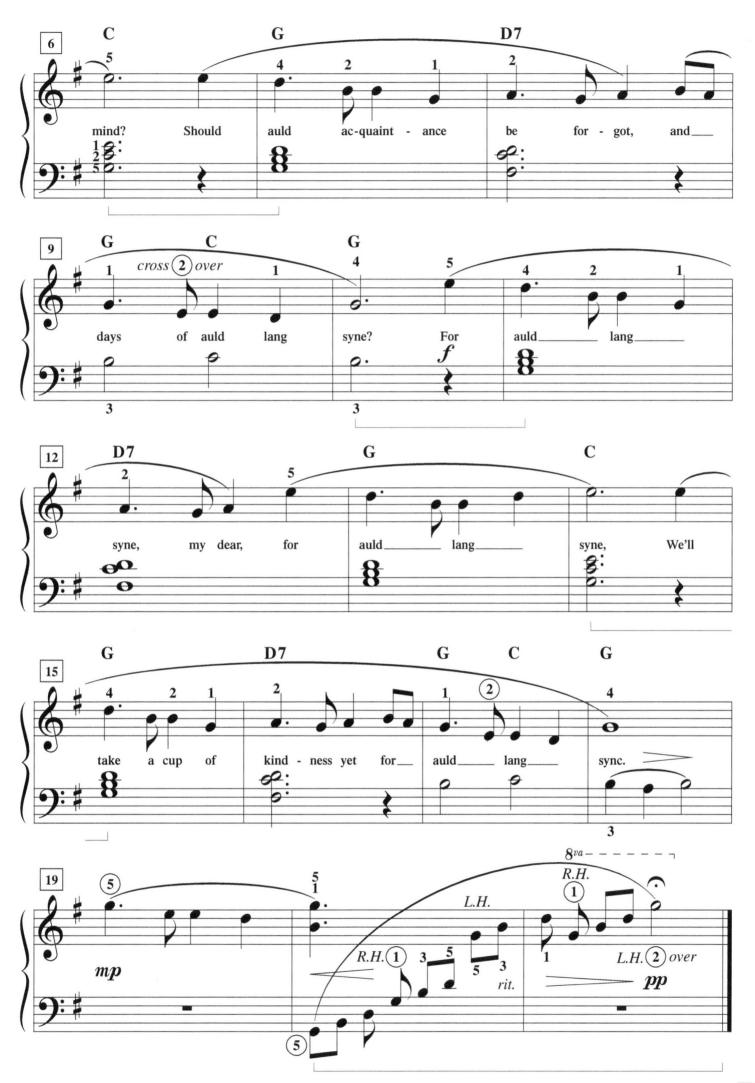

DICTIONARY OF MUSICAL TERMS
DYNAMIC MARKS

pp	*p*	*mp*	*mf*	*f*
pianissimo	*piano*	*mezzo piano*	*mezzo forte*	*forte*
very soft	soft	moderately soft	moderately loud	loud

crescendo (cresc.)
Play gradually louder.

diminuendo (dim.) or decrescendo (decresc.)
Play gradually softer.

SIGN	TERM	DEFINITION
	accent mark	Play this note louder.
	accidental	Sharps, flats, or naturals added to a piece and not in the key signature.
	C major chord	A three-note chord built in 3rds above C: C-E-G.
	C major scale	An eight-note scale (C-D-E-F-G-A-B-C) with half steps between scale steps 3-4 and 7-8.
	chord	Three or more tones sounding together.
	I ("one") chord	The Roman numeral I indicates the triad built on scale degree 1.
	IV ("four")	The Roman numeral IV indicates the triad built on scale degree 4.
	V7 ("five-seven")	A four-note chord built up in 3rds from scale degree 5 (often played with only three notes.)
	chord symbol	The letter name of a chord (shown above the staff) indicating the harmony.
	coda	Ending section.
	D7 chord	A four-note chord built up in 3rds from D (D-F♯-A-C). The notes of the D7 chord are often inverted to form a 3-note D7 chord.
D.C. al Fine	**Da Capo al Fine**	Return to the beginning and play until *Fine* (end).
D.S.	**Dal Segno**	Repeat from the 𝄋 sign.
	damper pedal	The right pedal, which sustains the sound, played with the right foot.
	dotted half note	Three counts or beats.
	eighth notes	Two eighth notes equal one quarter note.
	fermata	Hold this note longer than its normal value.
	fifth (5th)	The interval of a 5th spans five letter names. (Ex. C up to G, or A down to D) Line-(skip-a-line)-line, or space-(skip-a-space)-space.
	1st and 2nd endings	Play the 1st ending and repeat from the beginning. Then play the 2nd ending, skipping over the 1st ending.
	flat	A flat lowers a note one half step.
	fourth (4th)	The interval of a 4th spans four letter names. (Ex. C up to F, or G down to D) Line-(skip-a-line)-space, or space-(skip-a-space)-line.
	G major chord	A three-note chord built in 3rds above G: G B D. G is the root. B is the 3rd. D is the 5th.
	G major scale	An eight-note scale (G-A-B-C-D-E-F♯-G) with half steps between scale degrees 3-4 and 7-8.
	G7 chord	A four-note chord built up in 3rds from G (G-B-D-F). The notes of the G7 chord are often inverted to form a 3-note G7 chord.

	Term	Definition
♩	**half note**	Two counts or beats (one-half the value of a whole note).
	half rest	Two counts of silence. (Sits on line 3 of the staff)
	half step	The distance from one key to the very closest key on the keyboard. (Ex. C-C♯, or E-F)
	interval	The distance between two musical tones, keys on the keyboard, or notes on the staff. (Ex. 2nd, 3rd, 4th, 5th)
	key signature	The key signature appears at the beginning of each line of music. It indicates sharps or flats to be used throughout the piece.
	ledger line	A short line used to extend the staff.
	legato	Smooth, connected.
	major scale	An eight-note scale with half steps between scale degrees 3-4 and 7-8.
♮	**natural**	A natural (always a white key) cancels a sharp or a flat.
	octave	The interval which spans 8 letter names. (Ex. C to C)
8*va*	*ottava*	Play one octave higher (or lower) than written.
	pedal change	Shows the down-up motion of the damper pedal.
	phrase	A musical sentence. A phrase is often shown by a slur, also called a phrase mark.
	primary chords	The I, IV, and V chords are the primary chords in any major key.
♩	**quarter note**	One count or beat. (One-quarter the value of a whole note.)
♪	**quarter rest**	One beat of silence.
‖: :‖	**repeat sign**	Play the music within the repeat signs again.
rit.	*ritardando*	Gradually slowing down.
	root position	The letter name of the chord is the lowest note.
	scale	From the Latin word *scala*, meaning "ladder." The notes of a scale move up or down by 2nds (steps).
	second (2nd) (step)	The interval that spans two letter names. (Ex. C up to D, or F down to E) On the staff: line-to-the-next-space or space-to-the-next-line.
♯	**sharp**	A sharp raises the note one half step.
	sixth (6th)	The interval that spans six letter names. (Ex. E up to C) On the staff a 6th is written line-(skip 2 lines)-space or space-(skip 2 spaces)-line.
	slur	A curved line that indicates legato playing.
	staccato	Detached, disconnected.
	tempo	The speed of the music.
	third (3rd) (skip)	The interval that spans three letter names. (Ex. C up to E, or F down to D) On the staff: line-to-the-next-line or space-to-the-next-space.
	tie	A curved line that connects two notes on the same line or space. Hold for the total counts of both notes.
$\frac{3}{4}$ $\frac{4}{4}$	**time signature**	Two numbers at the beginning of a piece (one above the other). The top number indicates the number of beats per measure; the bottom number represents the note receiving the beat.
	triad	A 3-note chord built in 3rds.
	upbeat (pick-up note)	The note(s) of an incomplete opening measure.
o	**whole note**	Four counts or beats.
	whole rest	Silence for any whole measure. (Hangs below line 4)
	whole step	The distance of two half steps.

ALPHABETICAL INDEX OF TITLES